D0983791

PLATO'S *SYMPOSIUM*

Eros and the Human Predicament

TWAYNE'S MASTERWORK STUDIES

Robert Lecker, General Editor

PLATO'S *SYMPOSIUM*

Eros and the Human Predicament

Jamey Hecht
Castleton State College

TWAYNE PUBLISHERS
New York

Twayne's Masterwork Studies No. 173

Plato's *Symposium*: *Eros and the Human Predicament*
Jamey Hecht

Twayne Publishers
1633 Broadway
New York, NY 10019

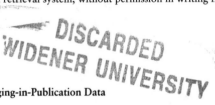

Library of Congress Cataloging-in-Publication Data
Hecht, Jamey.
  Plato's Symposium : Eros and the human predicament / Jamey Hecht.
    p.   cm. — (Twayne's masterwork studies ; no.173)
  Includes bibliographical references and index.
  ISBN 0-8057-1639-4 (alk. paper)
    1. Plato. Symposium.   2. Socrates.   3. Love.   I. Title
  II. Series.
  B385.H43   1999
  184—dc21   99-32694
                                                          CIP

10 9 8 7 6 5 4 3 2 1

Printed in the United States of America

To my sisters and to my parents

Contents

Preface

This book is part of the *Twayne's Masterwork Studies* series, a set of texts written for the undergraduate reader. I have used several of its volumes in my own teaching at various universities, and I feel privileged to contribute to an educational product that has proven so genuinely useful. One of the chief merits of the series is that each *Twayne's* book leads the student on to books of other kinds. Rather than simply explicate the title work, these studies tend to open out the field of history and criticism surrounding it. I have followed that practice here, and in addition to the selected bibliography at the end, I have referred to plenty of important good books, ancient and modern, in the notes.

I capitalize and italicize the word *Symposium* when it refers to the text and leave it lowercase in roman type to refer to the drinking party therein depicted. My chronology mixes literary dates with political and military-historical ones, since this seemed the best way to convey a unified, ongoing complex of events rather than several parallel but separate strands. In analyzing the speeches, I have broken each one down into a series of numbered points, so that easy reference can be made to the various logical moves of each speech. When these numbered points are in direct translation, as was often necessary, I have put them in quotation marks; where there are no such marks, the points are paraphrases. To prevent those convenient lists from becoming monotonous, I sometimes revert to quoted paragraphs. Translations are my own unless otherwise noted, and I have deliberately left these translations as literal as possible, so as not to obscure any available nuances of the Greek. The English is therefore a bit rough and unidiomatic, but I think this extra measure of fidelity is valuable in a heuristic book like this one. I call it heuristic (from the Greek *heurisko* [find]) because its purpose is to acquaint readers with the major issues of Plato's *Symposium,* so as to equip them in their own efforts to experience insight into this text and its subject, which is love. Like every exposition, this one makes some decisions about the text it investigates, but in keeping with the heuristic goal I have indicated, the commentary raises more questions than it answers.

Note on the References and Acknowledgments

In 1578 the French printer Henri Estienne II (now known by his Latinized surname, *Stephanus*) brought out a comprehensive edition of Plato's works. The page numbers of that edition were adopted as a standard system of reference to passages in the Platonic corpus. These Stephanus pages are broken down further into lettered sections, making it easier to use the "Stephanus numbers" to find a specific spot in the text. All modern editions of the Greek texts of Plato, and most translations, give these Stephanus numbers and letters in the margins. They have been used here in the notes and in the body of the text; it should be a simple matter for the reader to find a copy of *Symposium* that indicates these Stephanus numbers. In Stephanus's edition, *Symposium* occupied pages 172 to 223.

There is not much Greek in this quite introductory volume, though I have transliterated and defined a few salient terms; readers may ignore this dimension of the book if they like. Ancient Greek is a mighty intellectual resource and a profound life experience, and students of all disciplines—especially English, comparative literature, religious studies, sociology, linguistics, and history—should be encouraged to add it to their repertoires. Two important contributors to Ancient Greek literacy at the moment are the *Latin-Greek Institute* in New York City, which was founded in 1972 by Floyd Moreland and Rita Fleisher and which has been the model for many fine imitations throughout the country; and the *Perseus Project,* Tufts University's Internet database of Greek and Roman literature, edited by Gregory Crane. The author is grateful to the *Latin-Greek Institute,* especially to Hardy Hansen, David Sider, and Jack Collins, for their outstanding instruction. Theodore Korzukhin read an early draft of the manuscript and provided valuable suggestions and insight. I am also grateful to David Gallop for his critical acumen and advice. Any infelicities remain my own responsibility.

Several books have proven useful in the writing of this study, the most original and insightful being Stanley Rosen's monograph, *Plato's Symposium*. Like most students of this dialogue I have benefited from Rosen's full-length study, from K. J. Dover's 1980 edition of the Greek text, and from Martha Nussbaum's chapter on *Symposium* in *The Fragility of Goodness*. My reading of the Greek has also been aided by Gilbert Rose's Bryn Mawr Commentary, and the translations of R. E. Allen, Walter Hamilton, and Robin Waterfield. It is with gratitude that I repeat some of their insights in these pages.

Chronology

This chronology is indebted to that found in Charles Rowan Beye's *Greek Literature and Society*.[1] All dates are B.C.E., so that later dates bear smaller integers.

499	Ionian cities revolt from Persia with help from Athens and Eretria.
495	Pericles is born; Sophocles is born.
490	First Persian invasion of Greece is launched; Persians are defeated at Marathon.
487	Public officials at Athens are chosen by lot rather than by voting.
483	Athenians discover an abundant new vein of silver in the Laurium mine. Themistocles convinces the Assembly to fund a new fleet of ships.
480	Second Persian invasion of Greece is launched, a much larger one than that of 490. Battle of Thermopylae. Greek victory at Salamis.
479	Greek victories at Plataea and Mycale. Persians withdraw.
477	The Delian League is formed to preserve Greek security against Persia.
469	Socrates is born.
461	Pericles' dominance in the Assembly begins, ending with his death in 429.
431	The 27-year-long Peloponnesian War breaks out.
430	Plague breaks out in Athens.
429	Plato is born (d. 347 B.C.E.). Pericles dies. Cleon rises in the Assembly.
421	Alcibiades begins to dominate Athenian politics. Dramatic date of the drinking party in *Symposium*.

LITERARY AND
HISTORICAL CONTEXT

1

Historical Context

THE POLIS

The story of ancient Greece, and especially the story of its most important city, Athens, is about the rise and decline of a unique way of life based on the small-scale city-state, or *polis*. Our modern cities are enormous by comparison; while New York hosts maybe 8 million souls, Aristotle (384–322 B.C.E.) advised that in the ideal polis each citizen should be capable of knowing all the others by sight. We can suppose that this was more or less the case in fifth-century B.C.E. Athens, which at its peak had about 25,000 citizens, though the total population (including slaves and resident aliens) was much larger. Even so, Aristotle's suggestion was by no means idle; the great advantage of the polis way of life was the human scale of its undertakings and the directness of individual involvement in affairs both public and private. This business of knowing everybody else by sight means a great deal when the institutions of public life—the courts, the Assembly, religious festivals, and the military—are run by the people at large, rather than by specialized, trained professionals.

Athenian glory began with military victory (in 490 B.C.E. and again in 480 B.C.E.) over a non-Greek invader. It ended with defeat at the hands of the Spartans, a Doric Greek people whose highly regimented way of life was considered antithetical to Athenian ideals. The conflict with Sparta took decades to resolve, and by the time of the decisive Spartan victory in 404 B.C.E., Athens had lost its wealth, its naval preeminence, and much of its population. Along with all those lives, the war also destroyed that unique combination of stability and experiment that had animated the city at its height. Plato was born in 429 B.C.E., just as the Peloponnesian War began, and his writings reflect disillusion with the old Athenian ways in religion, politics, and education, since it seemed that under their guidance so much had been squandered and lost.

DEMOCRACY AND WOMEN

Around 510 B.C.E., with the fall of the monarch Peisistratos, the Athenian polis became a democracy. Property qualifications for holding office and membership in the Assembly were gradually removed, and those offices that had been electoral (with the exception of the military generalship) were now chosen by lot instead. Athens became, in the words of the British classicist H. D. F. Kitto, "as democratic as the ingenuity of man could make it."[1] But women had no political rights in this democracy, and though their lot cannot be imagined as thoroughly miserable strictly on the grounds that they lacked the specific prerogatives of their brothers, our admiration for the political achievements of the classical period should be tempered by that sober reflection. Not until the turn of the nineteenth century did women achieve political rights in most of the countries of the Western world, and this is generally understood as a legacy of Roman law. The Roman view of women inherited some salient features from classical Athenian culture, though these were ultimately transformed by Christianity. Despite its prevention of women's political existence, Athens can still be seen as the remote origin of Enlightenment ideals that eventually led to women's political emancipation in the modern world. Perhaps the central resemblance between classical and modern republics is their recourse to constitutionalism. Among its many functions, a constitution usually defines the category "citizen"—and this necessarily entails the opposite category "noncitizen." The history of women seems to show that their access to power was wider in the nonconstitutional societies, whose regimes of heredity and influence held sway between the end of the classical world and its resurgence in the revolutions of the eighteenth century. In the ancient world, it was Athens and its evolving constitution that realized the possibility of large-scale civic participation in national affairs.

THE PERSIAN WAR

As the Greek historian Herodotus pointed out, Athens could not have been more different from the Persian Empire across the Aegean Sea, where reigned a despot whose subjects worshiped him as a god. Persian power expanded westward toward the water, until some Greek colonies in Ionia, on the western shore of what is now Turkey, fell under the Persian yoke. When, with some help from the Athenians and from their neighbors the Eretrians, they revolted in 499 B.C.E., the Persian emperor Darius decided to punish not just the Ionian colonists but also their supporters across the Aegean. He sent a punitive expedition against Eretria and Athens in 490 B.C.E. Eretria was sacked, but the Persians did not reach Athens; amazingly, they were defeated by the grossly outnumbered Athenians at the battle of Marathon.[2]

Ten years later a second attempt was made, this time by Darius's son, the emperor Xerxes. This was the Persian War, whose progress forms the focus of Herodotus's *Histories.* Despite the vast scale of the invasion, the united Greeks were again victorious. In 477 B.C.E. Athens orchestrated the founding of a security organization, the Delian League, named for its base at the sacred island of Delos. At first this measure was popular, but discontent grew as the demands of the league became burdensome and the Persian threat seemed to fade. Three small states seceded from the league—Carystus in 472 B.C.E., Naxos in 470 B.C.E., and Thasos in 465 B.C.E.—and were promptly crushed. Other revolts against Athenian hegemony were put down in the years following, but perhaps the clearest sign of the shift from consensual alliance to compelled empire was the relocation of the league's treasury from Delos to Athens itself in 454 B.C.E.

PERICLES

The vicissitudes of Athenian policy in this 50-year period between the wars (Thucydides [ca.471–ca.400 B.C.E.] called it the *pentekontaetia*) are too many and complex to narrate here; suffice it to say that although it was sometimes prudent and even benevolent, Athens's behavior outraged her allies often enough to drive them to the Spartans for help. Athens was, we have said, ruled by the citizens in their own Assembly, but it is in the nature of such a body that gifted individuals can rise to prominence and even leadership through the recurrent opportunity to speak and be heard. Such an individual was Pericles. A democrat with a high aristocratic lineage, Pericles seemed to combine the values of the past and the present in a single figure. His brilliant oratory and strategic insight won him the Assembly's enduring respect and the political capital to direct the popular will—and even to rebuke the angry crowd when his judgment required it. For 30 years he more or less steered the city's course through the hazards of peace and war. The central policy of his career was restraint: Athens could keep her empire, Pericles assured the Assembly, but only if she refrained from (1) engaging the Spartans in major land battles and (2) attempting to expand the empire too quickly.[3]

THE PELOPONNESIAN WAR

In 432 B.C.E. a group of dissenting nations—bound by ties of kinship to the Spartans or simply irate at Athenian dominance—met at Sparta and decided to fight Athens. They occupied Attica (the region that surrounds the city proper), burning the farms and orchards, so that the local farmers and their families took shelter inside the city. This Pericles had anticipated; but he was entirely surprised by the plague that followed (430 B.C.E.), as thousands of these displaced peasants, along with citizens and slaves, sickened and died within the crowded city's walls. About a third of the Athenian soldiers perished.[4] The people blamed Pericles for the disaster and even fined him; though they later restored him to office, he died of the plague in 429 B.C.E. His successor as the major voice in the Assembly was Cleon (d. 422 B.C.E.), a man of some fortitude and cunning but without the charisma or the vision of Pericles. Where Pericles defied the reckless passions of popular sentiment, Cleon directly appealed to them.

Plato was born in the year of Pericles' death; his boyhood and youth saw the precarious balance of Athenian fortunes brought to its collapse. Political and military events combined to create the tragic downturn in Athens's fate: because they were losing the war, they suffered three oligarchic revolutions, each of which temporarily destroyed Athenian democracy and permanently weakened its credibility. Because of the political assassinations and loss of morale involved in these revolutions, Athens made more blunders in the war.

THE CAREER OF ALCIBIADES

The major figure in this period of decline is another aristocrat, Alcibiades (ca.450—404 B.C.E.) the son of Cleinias. The brief essay on his life by Plutarch (ca.45–ca.120 C.E.) is still a thrilling read, and he also figures prominently in Thucydides' account of the war. What makes him so important for our purposes is his friendship with Socrates and his appearance in *Symposium,* near the end of which Plato gives him one of the finest speeches in the dialogue. That speech is as vivid a portrait of the old philosopher as any we have, and it also captures much of the extraordinary charisma and strangeness of Alcibiades himself. Before turning to his relationship with Socrates, we should consider this man's career, since in its grandeur and its strange pathos it forms the heart of the next period in Athenian history.

After Pericles' death, his two injunctions were quickly forgotten: Athens lost a land engagement (one they might have avoided) at

Delium in 424 B.C.E., and another at Mantinea in 418 B.C.E. (Ehrenberg, 285). Then in 415 B.C.E. they made the grand, decisive mistake of the whole war: they attempted to invade the distant and massive island of Sicily, whose strength they had grossly underestimated. Nicias warned against it, but Alcibiades, the beautiful and ambitious young nobleman, easily outshone his elder fellow general, whose caution seemed outmoded and defeatist by comparison. The fleet was outfitted and everything was ready to go when the morning light revealed that, in this terribly sensitive moment, a sacrilegious outrage had been perpetrated: during the night, the statues of Hermes the Protector, which stood guard at Athenian houses, were partially smashed, their extremities broken off. This religious scandal, known in the scholarly literature as "the desecration of the Herms," is linked with a second sacrilegious affair, "the profanation of the Mysteries," in which Alcibiades and his friends were accused of reenacting the sacred and secret rites of Eleusinian Demeter in his private home, in front of noninitiates. These rites were of the greatest religious importance, and it was a matter of prodigious hubris that anyone should dare to perform them—let alone mock them—beyond the confines of the temple at Eleusis.

Alcibiades, who had done plenty of shocking things in the past (though nothing so frighteningly transgressive as this), was accused, but the urgency and popularity of the imminent expedition moved the court to postpone his trial until the end of the campaign. So Alcibiades sailed off to Sicily, far more eager for the fight than Nicias and far more gifted for its direction than the third general, Lamachus. In his absence, the people grew resentful, and they recalled him to the city to stand trial—interrupting his work. This infuriated him, and in response to it he did the unthinkable: He defected to Sparta, where he divulged valuable military secrets, and even encouraged the Spartans to set up a permanent garrison near Athens—a thing they might never have done on their own and that proved crucial to their eventual victory. He also informed the Spartans of the state of things in Sicily, with the result that the capable Spartan commander Gulippus was dispatched there to fight off the Athenians, which he did with resounding success. Outdone by Gulippus and intimidated by an ominous eclipse of the moon, Nicias squandered an opportunity for safe retreat, and a massacre ensued. This episode forms one of the most moving and tragic passages in Thucydides' *Peloponnesian War*; by the end of the expedition, Nicias is executed by allies of the Spartans, while the marooned and leaderless Athenians starve to death at the bottom of a quarry.

After this prodigious service to the Spartans, Alcibiades undertook a friendship with an important Persian official, whose considerable wealth and power he employed to play the Spartans and the Athenians against one another. He seems to have taken stock of the situation during this interlude and found that he might return to Athenian affairs after all. An oligarchic revolution broke out in Athens in 411 B.C.E. When word of this reached the troops of the Athenian citizen-army in the field, they were furious, since they were risking their lives in the name of a democracy that had been sabotaged in their absence. They called upon Alcibiades to lead them home and restore it. Instead, he led them in some valuable strategic fights in the eastern Aegean, right where they were. Back at home, the oligarchy was overthrown within a few months, during which time Alcibiades and his new men achieved stunning victories over the Spartans and their allies. He was summoned back to Athens in glory, his ships decked with the captured figureheads of almost two hundred enemy vessels.

After a short stay in his native polis he set out again to reconquer Ionia. He soon discovered that the Persians, with their vast wealth, were now firmly on the side of Sparta and that this was the result of talented new Spartan leadership in the person of the admiral Lysander. For his part Alcibiades was running out of money, and he repeatedly had to leave the action in order to raise more. At the start of one such voyage, he made the mistake of entrusting the command to a personal friend, with the proviso that he not risk a full battle in Alcibiades' absence. But like Patroclus in the *Iliad,* who insisted on confronting Hector himself though Achilles had warned him not to do so, the friend disobeyed and was ruined, along with at least 15 ships, in a naval fight at Notium near Ephesus in 407 B.C.E.

Because of his subordinate's mistake—for which Alcibiades was, after all, officially responsible—the Athenians dealt Alcibiades the second major insult of his career: they refused to reelect him general in 406 B.C.E. His successors were distinctly inferior to both Lysander the Spartan and to Alcibiades, whose timely advice they contemptuously rejected at the peril of their men's lives. Lysander conquered them in fairly short order, and within two years the Peloponnesian War was over. Sparta dictated the terms of the Athenian surrender and barely prevented her allies, Thebes and Corinth, from sacking the city itself. Alcibiades, who had fled to the court of another old Persian associate, was murdered by Persian agents on the advice of Lysander in 404 B.C.E., just as Athens herself was dying.

Most readers despise Alcibiades when they first learn of his temporary defection to Sparta with its disastrous results for the Sicilian expedition. It must be remembered, however, that the Athenians themselves prevented him from finishing what he started in Sicily. They accused him of the desecration of the Herms on evidence that is still regarded as little better than hearsay, and for a penalty they first confiscated his estate, then had the priests and priestesses of the city pronounce curses upon him, and finally condemned him to death in absentia. Though these punishments were later reversed, their effect on Alcibiades was clearly quite serious. When the city denounced him the second time, he left the campaign and settled into one of his residences nearby; but he nevertheless warned the generals who had replaced him that their position was exposed and that the Spartans on the facing shore had superior discipline in camp. He did not have to give that advice, and the fact that he did—*after* he had been insulted—indicates that, at least at that late date, he may have grown beyond the radically individualistic opportunism that characterized so much of his career.

Here is the statement of Plutarch, a historian writing several centuries after the fact, on the Athenians' regret over their dismissal of Alcibiades in 406 B.C.E.:

> The loss of their supremacy dealt a terrible blow to the spirit of the Athenians. But when Lysander went on to deprive them of their freedom as well and handed over the city to the Thirty Tyrants, their eyes began to be opened—now that their affairs were irretrievably ruined—to the various actions they had failed

to take while it was still in their power to save themselves. In their despair they recalled their past mistakes and follies, and they considered that the greatest of all had been their second outburst against Alcibiades. They had thrown him aside through no fault of his own, but simply because they were angry with one of his subordinates for having disgraced himself and lost a few ships, yet they themselves had behaved far more disgracefully in depriving the city of the finest and most experienced general they possessed.[5]

This man represents the end of the fifth century B.C.E.; he is an aristocrat with claims to the noble past, but he prizes his own personal excellence as the basis of his extraordinary individual value. Though he was raised in the house of his relative Pericles and was (however abortively) taught temperance by Socrates, he remained an impulsive, vain, mercurial figure, readily comparable to the god Hermes against whose statues he was accused of committing outrage. Though he used his prodigious gifts to help his native city, he also deliberately helped the enemy when Athens had hurt his feelings. Extraordinarily beautiful, eloquent, and intelligent, Alcibiades seems to have had a transgressive streak in his nature that is often adduced as an indicator of the breakdown of Athenian social cohesion—one compares Alcibiades to, say, his guardian Pericles and is struck by the younger man's thoroughly individualistic outlook. But Pericles and the fifth century B.C.E. efflorescence for which he stands were largely the product of an education in Homer, the eighth century B.C.E. poet whose *Iliad* and *Odyssey* were memorized by Greek students with the fervor of pioneer Americans memorizing their King James Bible.[6] As Pericles' "Funeral Oration" declares, Athens is the preeminent "School of Hellas" (the cultural teacher of all Greece) because she motivates each man to strive for his own form of excellence using his own natural endowments (whereas in Sparta, each citizen is engaged in communal, regimented military training from age 6 to 60). Homer provides the basis for that kind of initiative because his heroes embody the aristocratic values of the Archaic period, each hero bent on increasing his own personal fame (or *kleos*) through valor on the battlefield. Achilles, the hero of the *Iliad,* even abandons his own army and very effectively prays for its destruction rather than compromise his own wounded honor. This is precisely what Alcibiades did, and depending on our own needs we can construe his action as the tragic onset of Hellenistic[7] decadence or as a last flowering of aristocracy and Homeric heroism. Indeed, because of Alcibiades' appetite for popular acclaim (see *Symposium* 216b5), Plato sometimes seems to suggest that it was the democracy itself that produced him and his excesses.

THE CAREER OF SOCRATES

Socrates' trial, described in the Platonic dialogue called the *Apology*, shows the old man debating with his accusers about the meaning of his career as a seeker of knowledge. While we usually read that work for its insights about virtue and education, we also learn a great deal about the Athenian political environment in this period from the fact that so eloquent a defendant was nevertheless condemned to drink poison.

RHETORIC

Another feature of late fifth century B.C.E. Athenian life prominent in both *Apology* and *Symposium* is the increasing importance of the art of rhetoric in public and private affairs. Professional rhetors charged fees in exchange for polished speeches that their clients used for defense or prosecution in the courts. As Greek civic institutions developed, and urban life took on a certain world-weariness, people began to sue each other more often.[8] While there is practically no point in suing a poor person, and there were penalties for initiating a suit and then losing it, Socrates was a special case: A poor man with rich friends, he was resented in part because of the political intrigues of his former students and associates, in part because of his own difficult and sometimes irritating questions. Socrates' eloquence was not the same as what the Sophists sold, and he often (e.g., in *Gorgias, Protagoras*) used it to expose Sophistry as a kind of gimmick, unworthy of being called an art (*technê*) like music or poetry. But other defendants and plaintiffs, who lacked this eloquence, needed all the gimmickry they could afford, and Athenian culture was irreversibly transfigured by the advent of *rhetorikê technê* and the cynicism and anxiety it generated among rhetoricians, Sophists, and their conservative detractors.[9]

The courts were the arena in which persuasive rhetoric was employed in the attack and defense of private interests, while the public interest was advanced in the *Ecclesia,* or Assembly. There, free citizens (who grew more numerous as the property qualifications for citizenship were gradually removed) vied with one another over the possible courses of action in governing Athenian affairs. Because this democracy is the proudly adduced ancestor of various modern claimants to the name, it is easy to forget some of the salient differences: our democracies are representative; for the most part, theirs was not. Any citizen who could speak could do so in the Assembly, and if he spoke well enough, his rhetoric might change the nation's strategy in war or its ambitions in peace. Under such a regime the benefits of a silver tongue are substantial, easily worth the few hundred drachmas charged by a good Sophist for a rhetorical education.[10]

If such well-organized, monologic speeches form an important part of Plato's work, the rest of it is dialogic question and answer, or "dialectic"—the distinctive mode of discourse used by the historical Socrates to probe the minds of his interlocutors and to approach the truth of whatever he happened to be concerned with. Socrates was quite consciously committed to dialectic, and Plato portrays him insisting on its use whenever his conversation partners threaten to break off the exchange with longer, Sophistic speeches. Sometimes Socrates makes such a speech himself or recounts the speech of someone else he admires (for instance, Diotima in *Symposium*), and when he does so, it is worth taking account of the special shift away from his usual practice.

Although the term *dialectic* originally referred to Socrates' technique of question and answer, the nineteenth-century C.E. philosopher Georg Wilhelm Friedrich Hegel used the same word to refer to something quite different, and the term was given a further spin by Karl Marx's appropriation of Hegel later in the same century. It is important to keep this distinction in mind, though context usually makes it quite clear whether the word on somebody's page is the Platonic one or the almost-unrelated term from German Idealism.[11]

DIALOGUE

A *genre* is a set of texts having in common certain parameters of subject and form; the adjective form of the noun *genre* (adopted from the French) is *generic*. Plato had generic precedents for his philosophical dialogues, the most substantial of which were the tragic and comic dramas of the Athenian theater. Less famous, but perhaps as personally compelling, were the dialogues of that Simon the Cobbler whose very shop seems to have been recently excavated in the marketplace of the old city. Diogenes Laertius, the third century C.E. author of *Lives of Eminent Philosophers,* tells us that this Simon was said to be "the first to recount Socrates' conversations in dialogue form."[12] Diogenes later gives a formulation that still strikes us as particularly apt: "But in my view Plato ought to be awarded the prize of priority both for discovery and for the beauty of the genre, since he brought it to its perfection" (Kerferd, 33).

Indeed, Plato developed the written dialogue so successfully that, by comparison, no other philosopher's use of the dialogue form quite seems adequate: Plato is to philosophical dialogue what Shakespeare is to the five-act dramatic-verse play. Though Socrates himself wrote nothing down, Plato's dialogues blend the illusion of spontaneous conversation among multiple speakers with the reality of meticulous literary work by the single writer, Plato himself.[13] But *Symposium* also belongs to a smaller subgenre, the speculative dinner conversation. Contemporary and later writers followed Plato in occasionally setting philosophical discussions in domestic environments where ritual eating and drinking were going on. This device, while depicting a real institution of upper-class Athenian life, lends the conversation a warmth and informality that keeps the speakers human, making it easier for a reader to identify with them (and perhaps even with the positions they take).

Dialectic was not Socrates' only innovation; the most striking feature of the movement that bears his name was a new concern with ethics. The writers we call pre-Socratics were, for the most part, profoundly poetic thinkers who investigated the sensible (that is, perceptible by the senses) aspects of the cosmos. They also speculated on the origin of the world and the relationship of mankind to the gods, and their writings about nature often had deep metaphysical implications.[14] One of them, Anaxagoras, had the young Socrates as a pupil, and in his eventual break with his teacher, Socrates understood himself to be shifting from physics, or the study of nature, to ethics, the study of human action. At any rate, he came to demand that such interest as we take in the physical phenomena of nature ought to be limited to the insight they can give us into ethics. For example, there is a passage in Plato's *Ion* in which the process of reciting epic poetry is compared to the way a magnet causes a heap of iron rings to form a hanging chain, communicating the attractive force from ring to ring. Socrates has no interest in magnetism in its own right, and he appeals to it in the *Ion* only because of its usefulness in explaining something else, namely, the ethical issues of rhapsody: the relationship obtaining among Muse, Poet, Rhapsode, and Audience—which relationship happens to be perfectly expressed in the magnet analogy.[15]

In keeping with this ethical focus, Socrates refused to accept fees for his "teaching," explicitly denying that his conversations constituted a teaching or that he was himself a teacher. The Sophists teach a skill (namely, persuasive speaking), so it is reasonable that they should charge a fee. But Socrates searches for the truth and openly avows his own ignorance of it (e.g., in *Apology*), so he can hardly ask for money from those who simply wish to join him on the search. The only sense in which Socrates does seem to have felt himself deserving of reward was as a kind of social critic, since his ignorant but insightful prodding kept some of his contemporaries from the illusion that they were wise. *Apology* relates the striking anecdote of the oracle, which said that there was no one wiser than Socrates. Since Socrates was already long engaged in the business of stripping away false wisdom from his fellow Athenians, he took the oracle to be saying that while others were ignorant and falsely thought themselves wise, he at least had the wisdom to recognize his own ignorance.

After antiquity, Christian readers of Plato often regarded their religion as the missing knowledge that Socrates lacked. Such a gesture was not a failed effort to interpret the text on Plato's own terms— Christian interpreters also read Virgil's fourth Eclogue as an announcement of Christ's imminent arrival and, of course, read the entire Hebrew Bible as little more than a superseded preface to the New Testament. To the hermeneutic reader, such seemingly willful distortions are outrageous, a form of vandalism. But as we are sometimes reminded, life is deeper and wider even than scholarship, and no text can be fully understood unless we come to it with the awareness that texts, too, grow and change with the evolving demands of life upon humankind.

Fittingly, that awareness is itself a legacy of Plato. In the *Iliad*, Hector openly tells his wife that he is doomed to fall in the battle, because he shares with the audience a knowledge of the overarching story in which he finds himself. This shared knowledge is poignant, heartbreaking, solemn, but not ironic; there is no tension between what Hector knows of the eventual outcome and what we know. In Plato, history is what makes the difference between our full knowledge of the outcome and the characters' limited knowledge of it: The dialogues are generally set in the past, so that we see and hear Socrates and Agathon and Alcibiades and other long dead persons happily carousing in the explicit hope that their lives might turn out well, justice might be served, Athens might appreciate them, when Plato knew those hopes had already been disappointed in the meantime.

Irony like that is partly an inheritance of the tragic drama (in which the ignorant Oedipus curses "the criminal" to an audience that knows what he does not know, namely, that Oedipus *is* the guilty one). But what makes for the special emotional flavor of this Platonic irony is the way that history, rather than myth, supplies the outcome, known to writer and audience but unknown to the characters. Historians like Herodotus and Thucydides had already used this kind of historical irony for their own historiographical purposes. But in Plato, the real Athens and the fates of its inhabitants are the mere furniture of philosophical discussions that transcend the particulars of Socrates' death, Alcibiades' rise and fall—even Athens's loss of the Peloponnesian War is, in the bright light of philosophy, just another instance of all-too-human folly chasing the wrong object of desire. That is why the dialogues *can* be read without the accompanying historical background: The background helps, since Plato's irony deliberately exploits it for dramatic effect, but it is not strictly necessary, because that same irony reduces the historical material to the background.

Part of the sweet pain of reading this author closely is receiving just this set of mixed signals: On the one hand, Plato seems committed to the local and particular details of these characters, this setting, these gestures and faces—after all, he evokes them in such memorable ways, and they so frequently encode significant addenda to his arguments. On the other hand, his whole project is directed toward freeing us from our attachment to lovable particulars, thereby protecting us from their claim on our attention and from the possibility of their painful loss.[16] Everyone in the Socratic circle, including Plato, lost his mentor in 399 B.C.E., and as we hear from Alcibiades at 221c, "one searches and finds nobody even close [that is, similar] to him." For Plato, that experience may have been central in driving home the awful precariousness of human happiness as we know it and inciting him to the kind of voyage of ascent he urges upon us in Diotima's discourse at 205–212.

2

Critical Reception

Plato came to think that beyond the five senses and the world of ordinary reality that they disclose to us, there must be an imperishable reality to which we can only have access through the intellect. At various stages of his philosophical career he formulated this idea in several different ways, perhaps the most beautiful of which is to be found in Diotima's instructions to Socrates near the end of *Symposium*. Plato's evolving confidence in the Forms made regular, sense-related knowledge seem trivial by comparison, especially later in the Neoplatonist tradition (which pervaded both Christianity and Judaism), when the connection between the world of forms and the immortality of the soul became more explicit and, in the breakdown of the old, polis-centered way of life, more culturally urgent.

There is no codified, systematic statement of the Theory of Forms in Plato;[1] the account in *Symposium* differs from those of *Phaedrus* and *Republic,* for instance, and in parts of the *Theaetetus* and *Parmenides* Plato seems almost ready to abandon the theory altogether. But it was this theoretical and otherworldly aspect of Plato's thought that was taken up and developed most actively in succeeding centuries. Plotinus (205–270 C.E.) built onto it an edifice of speculative cosmology and metaphysics that owed a great deal to *Symposium* (though it owed even more to later Platonic dialogues like *Timaeus*). In turn, Plotinus's work was hugely influential in the doctrinal development of the early Church (despite Plotinus's personal contempt for Christianity) since it provided Christians with an intellectual basis for their faith. Its special merit in that capacity was Hellenization; the earliest Christianity was, remember, a largely Jewish affair whose context struck the Greek speakers of the Mediterranean as quite alien and even absurd. Steeping the faith in Plotinus meant remaking it for the Hellenistic mind, and at the root of that process, much reified and vulgarized, there lay Plato's brilliant and bizarre set of opinions about the Forms.

THE LEGACY OF PLATONISM

In an area sacred to the hero Academus, sometime between 380 and 365 B.C.E., Plato founded a permanent institution called the Academy. This seems to have been a place for discussion and teaching, though in Plato's lifetime no fees were charged for attendance. Plato was its first leader, or *scholarch,* and upon his death he designated his nephew Speusippus as his successor.[2] The scholarchy of the Academy passed in a line of succession for more than eight centuries, until 529 C.E., when the Christian Roman emperor Justinian (483–565 C.E.) ordered it closed (in accordance with a more general edict forbidding the teaching of philosophy in Athens). But this new dominance of Christianity only changed the course of Plato's influence, which has never ceased.

Saint Augustine of Hippo (354–430 C.E.) made Neoplatonism and Christianity inseparable, partly because his own personal development had led him from the one to the other, and he could only accomplish that development by working out a relationship between the two. The *Confessions* and *City of God* teem with residual Neoplatonism from Augustine's earlier life, and though he rejected what seemed to him to be contrary to Christian teaching, he acknowledged an intellectual debt to Platonic thought and its theistic striving to know the divine.

The influence of Plato's sometime student Aristotle grew steadily through most of the medieval period—especially after the establishment, around 1150 C.E., of schools for translation in Sicily and in the Spanish city of Toledo.[3] But the texts handled at these schools were already pervaded by an admixture of quite ancient Neoplatonism, which the scholars at Toledo were in no position to extricate or even identify as non-Aristotelian. Later, Thomas Aquinas (1225–1274 C.E.) assembled a coherent synthesis of Christian doctrine with the Aristotelian wisdom preserved and transmitted by Muslim and Jewish thinkers. As Plato's textual corpus began to reemerge during the late Middle Ages and the Renaissance, the official dogmas of the Church often defined themselves in explicit opposition to Plato. While some concessions were made to the claims of Platonic thought, he often functioned as the great opponent of doctrinaire Aristotelians, who had to meet his attested or imagined objections to their own positions.

The poet Dante (1265–1321 C.E.), despite a great devotion to Thomistic thought and its Aristotelian basis, found it necessary to concede several difficult philosophical and cosmological questions to Plato (e.g., the return of the soul to its star in *Paradiso* 4). More generally, Dante's conception of the soul's upward journey toward transcendent truth is partly an inheritance of the Jacob's Ladder image in Genesis 28:12, but its real antecedent is Diotima's discourse in *Symposium*. For Dante as for most medieval writers, the *Timaeus* was the most influential of Plato's works, because it was available to Western readers in a Latin version for most of the millennium when little else of Plato could be read by Europeans outside a handful of monasteries.

In the humanism of the Italian fourteenth and fifteenth centuries, the generations following Dante made an even more bold return to the Platonic tradition. Renaissance figures including Petrarch (1304–1374 C.E.) and Marsilio Ficino looked to Plato and Platonism for the roots of their own ambitions and a legitimation of their dissent from Thomist orthodoxy. In a similar way, some central ideas of the nineteenth-century romantic movement had been kept alive and available by intermittent Platonic revivals like that of the Cambridge Platonists in the latter half of the seventeenth century.[4]

Friedrich Nietzsche (1844–1900 C.E.) made a revolutionary gesture when he emphasized the damage Socrates did in depriving people of their illusions. At the same time, he attacked the Neoplatonic tradition and its intellectual legacy in Immanuel Kant (1724–1804 C.E.)

and Arthur Schopenhauer (1788–1860 C.E.), arguing that the pursuit of the "next world" left the current world languishing in a chronic cultural malaise. With frequent recourse to medical rhetoric, Nietzsche contrasted the world-weary, ascetic ethos of medieval life with the vitality and charm of the Renaissance, whose demise he persuasively blamed on the Christian Reformation. In the same spirit, he celebrated pre-Christian Rome and pre-Platonic Greece, so far unspoiled by the contagion of the Theory of Ideas and its more virulent Christian derivatives. If Socrates helped destroy the illusions that had made Greek culture so valuable for life, Plato had put in their place what was, for Nietzsche, the most pernicious illusion in history.[5]

Generations have been inspired by the scene of Socrates cheerfully awaiting execution in the hope that death might clarify the mysteries of existence. We moderns, for whom disillusion is perhaps the most salient feature of our cultural experience, tend to see the same scene as a warning: the search for certainty leads to death.

The subject of Plato's *Symposium* is love, several kinds of which are contrasted as each of seven dinner guests attempts to offer an encomium, or praise speech, in honor of Eros, the Greek god of love. The *Symposium*'s role in literary history has been shaped by the prominence of homosexuality in the dialogue's description of male erotic response. In particular, the sexual relationship between men and male adolescents, or paiderasty,[6] occupies a major place in the first half of the dialogue. With the waning of the Athenian context in which *Symposium* was written, its (qualifiedly sympathetic) treatment of this theme has come to seem culturally remote to many readers. But in general, this dialogue continues to exert a strong claim on the readership of the humanities because of the grandeur and the wisdom found in its conclusion. The next-to-last speech, that of Socrates, concerns the way our experience of beauty leads us out of our local concerns and attachments and into a vivid, participatory relationship with the sources of the phenomenal world. The final speech, that of Alcibiades, recounts anecdotes about Socrates himself that constitute our most vivid portrait of this enigmatic and originary figure, whose ethical power and intellectual invention continue to define our institutions, as much in their stability as in their evolution.

A READING

3

The Prologue (172a–174a)

It makes sense to consider the opening of *Symposium* a kind of prologue, since the bulk of the piece is taken up by the proceedings of the party in the title, whereas this opening scene is quite distinctly set off from it in time, place, and dramatis personae. Plato wrote *Symposium* around 383 B.C.E., but its dramatic date is much earlier: often understood to be the year 404 B.C.E.,[1] it is the moment when Apollodorus and his unnamed acquaintances (the "you" in the first sentence) are to be imagined holding the conversation that starts the piece. In the course of that conversation, Apollodorus recounts the speeches from a drinking party that took place 15 years before: the host, Agathon, had just won the tragedy competition at the Lenaean Festival of 416 B.C.E. This places the festivities one year prior to the disastrous Sicilian expedition. The Alcibiades we meet here is young and ambitious, at the earlier and greater of the two peaks of his prominence in public life. He and Agathon are each at a zenith that neither will attain again. Our symposium is the smaller, private affair on the night *after* the big cast party of his Lenaean victory. That is why the speechmakers are all, in varying degrees, hung over as they make their speeches about Eros.[2]

Eros and eros

Translations of *Symposium* usually manifest a certain tension between "Eros" (the named mythological figure) and "eros" (which refers to the love of some thing or practice but also to sexual desire, sexuality, and love between persons). This is due to the typographical conventions of English, since lowercase letters, accent marks, and punctuation were invented long after Plato wrote. Each speaker tries to construct a mythology of the god that will support the speaker's claims about the emotion.

As our reading proceeds, and the personal outlook of each speaker emerges, it is easy to lose sight of the controlling presence of Plato behind the scenes, ironically setting one speaker over against another and poetically setting into relief the foibles and the gifts of each member of this extraordinary gathering. The participants represent various aspects of the human predicament and the career of erotic desire—for example, the older man whose erotic needs outlive his beauty; the physician whose experience of love is complicated (if not diminished) by medical knowledge; the young poet whose sudden success casts a rosy glow over all he sees. Plato's art is such that we seem to hear seven distinct speakers in what we forget are the pages of a single, masterful hand.

But before we reach the speeches themselves, the prologue shows us an elaborate chain of storytellers:

1. Circa 404 B.C.E., some "men of wealth" ask Apollodorus about the 416 B.C.E. symposium;

2. Apollodorus replies that he just recounted the whole story to Glaucon the other day;

3. Glaucon had heard it already, in an unreliable form, from someone else,

4. who had been told about it by Phoenix son of Philip. Phoenix had heard it from

5. Aristodemus, who was present in 416 B.C.E. But Aristodemus has also told it to

6. Apollodorus, who has since confirmed the story in consultation with Socrates.

Only then do we get Apollodorus's narration of what Aristodemus told him and that Socrates confirmed. What might be the significance of this chain of storytellers? First, it evokes the past, showing how thin is the thread connecting contemporary Athens to the glorious Athens of 416 B.C.E. As an element of the text's genre, the chain of storytellers is a self-conscious reflection on the already rich tradition of reportage surrounding the conversations of Socrates and his associates, of which *Symposium* is only one example. Finally, it provides a comparison with the process by which human beings learn the truths of love. Each storylearner in the chain has made passing use of whatever story-knower he could find, gotten the story from him, and so become a storyteller in turn. This resembles the way the lovers in Diotima's instructions to Socrates (201d–212a) make use of each other to acquire the truth of love that, once learned, obviates the commitment to any particular lover just as the storytellers can leave behind their particular informants.

NOSTALGIA

Let us reflect further on the evocation of the past. Apollodorus's tale, and thereby the whole *Symposium,* begins with the shouted mention of Phalerum. This was "the original port-city of Athens, largely super-seded by Piraeus,"[3] so its name, too, must have stood for a lost past (rather like the way the names of some modern cities evoke their lost but once glorious powers—industrial for Pittsburgh or Cleveland, political for Boston or St. Petersburg). The ultimate expression of this looking backward is the myth of Aristophanes' speech, which depicts a time before history, when mankind was newly born. Those times past are immeasurably distant from the present, but the 416 B.C.E. sympo-sium is just distant enough to make dispassionate recollection of it somewhat difficult and a little complicated—not only because of the hazards of transmission (which we all know about from playing the "telephone" game as children) but also because of nostalgia. Consider this ambiguous line in the dramatic setting at 173a5: *hote tê prôtê tragôdia enikêsen Agathôn.* This phrase, which K. J. Dover offsets with commas in his edition of the Greek text, can be construed in at least two ways, and Plato's ambiguity seems to be quite deliberate. Either it simply means that Agathon won the victory *with his first tragedy,* or Apollodorus calls this occasion the *first* time Agathon won the victory in the tragedy competition.[4] *It was also the only time.*[5] Speaking in 404 B.C.E., Apollodorus has just been told that it is "a long time since Agathon lived in Athens"; therefore it is unlikely that (1) Agathon could have been expected by anyone in 404 B.C.E. to gain any further victories at the Athenian Lenaea, or that (2) Apollodorus could have forgotten that Agathon was triumphant only once. But the moment is one of recollection, the conjuring of a distant time "when we were boys yet," still on the naive, abundant, receiving end of the love of men, and not the experienced, hungry, pursuing end. In 416 B.C.E. the war might still have been won, the Sicilian expedition had not taken place, and Alcibiades, for his part, had not yet even been elected general. The slip, if it is a slip, concerning Agathon's "first" victory seems natural enough if we reflect that Apollodorus is a man of nostalgia, capable of waxing reminiscent even about events he did not witness, so long as they involve his beloved master Socrates. Whatever we think about this *character's* strange use of the word *protê* (first) for something that only happened once, *Plato's* use of it here has an ironic overtone that bears in upon us the world of possibilities, erotic, military, and political, that had been scintillating in 416 B.C.E. but was quite gone in 384 B.C.E. The atmosphere being recollected, that of 416 B.C.E., belongs with the feeling that Agathon's career, brilliantly begun, might remain brilliant—as Socrates puts it, Agathon's wisdom is "bright and full of promise" (175e).

FANATICISM

To recollect that atmosphere with the intellect alone would protect one from making this sort of misleading remark (not quite a mistake: it *was* his first victory), but Apollodorus is the last person we should expect to find capable of this. His fanaticism makes him a more accurate witness—"making it my business to know each day what Socrates says and does"—but this very fanaticism makes him get things strangely wrong at the same time. Socrates went shoeless out of an ongoing, light-hearted disregard for the body and for sartorial convention. Apollodorus, on the contrary, is passionate about shoelessness. When Socrates goes to a dinner party, he quite naturally makes an exception from his usual habits and appears bathed, oiled, and shod, but Apollodorus, who is merely imitating Socrates, is "always the same."

Here is Apollodorus's account of himself, from the recounted exchange with Glaucon on the dialogue's first page:

> "Whoever explained it to you evidently didn't do so at all clearly, if you believe that this gathering you're asking about took place recently, so that I could have been present at it."
>
> "Yes, I did think that," he said.
>
> "Where did you get that notion, Glaucon?" I asked. "Don't you know that Agathon hasn't lived here [in Athens] for many years, and it is not yet three years since I've been consorting with Socrates and have been making it my business each day to know what he says and does? Before then, I ran around in whatever direction I happened upon, believing I was accomplishing something, when I was more wretched than anyone—no worse off than you are now, thinking it necessary to do anything rather than philosophize." (172b–173a)

The problem with Apollodorus's newfound sense of mission is that it is devoted to Socrates, rather than to philosophy (let alone to wisdom itself).

Aristodemus also puts on Socratic manners; he is described as "a short man, always shoeless." This phrase is sometimes translated "little man," and the Greek seems to have this overtone: to be *always* shoeless, as an outward token of one's inner philosophical commitment, is to be ethically small—especially if one believes that by wearing no shoes one enhances one's greatness.

SOCRATES AS AN ODYSSEUS FIGURE: THE FIRST PROVERB

Here is Socrates' conversation with Aristodemus, who shares Apollodorus's Socratic affectations ("always shoeless").

And he answered, "I'm going to dinner at Agathon's. Yesterday I fled the victory-celebrations, for fear of the crowd, but I agreed to be there the next day. That is why I have beautified myself, to be beautiful as I go to the house of a beautiful man. But you," he said, "How do you feel about being willing to come uninvited to dinner?"

And so I [Aristodemus] said, "Whatever you say."

"Follow, then" said Socrates, "in order that we may distort the proverb, changing it, so that '*Good men come of their own accord to the feasts of good men.*' For Homer runs the risk not only of distorting the proverb, but of committing hubris against it: for, making Agamemnon a remarkably good man with respect to the things of warfare [sometimes translated, "a good general"], and Menelaus 'a feeble spear-fighter,' when Agamemnon is sacrificing and hosting a feast he [Homer] has Menelaus willingly attend the meal—being a worse man attending the meal of his better." (174a–c)

There are several things we should bear in mind here:

1. The proverb's usual form, which occurs, for instance, in fragment 289 of the comic poet Eupolis, is "*Good men go of their own accord to* bad *men's feasts.*"
2. There are two parallelisms: the first is a pair of uses of the word *kalos,* "to be *beautiful* as I go to the house of a *beautiful* man"; the second is a pair of uses of the word *agathos,* in the proverb: "*Good* men come of their own accord to the feasts of *good* men."
3. This use of *agathos* is itself a pun on the name of the host, Agathon.

The relationship between the beautiful and the good is an important issue in the group of dialogues to which *Symposium* belongs, but it has a much more explicit role to play in *Republic* or *Phaedrus* than in *Symposium*. The main action of these lines is Socrates reassuring Aristodemus that it is okay to come along uninvited. But Socrates does not quite follow through with this reassurance: at first he says (using another proverb, to which we will turn in a moment) that they will both come up with an excuse for Aristodemus as they walk together on their way to the party, but then Socrates lags behind, lost in his own thoughts, and bids his friend go on ahead. We are never told what it was that so preoccupied Socrates that he had to arrive late, but we do learn later that he stood in the neighbor's doorway for a long time, motionless.

Since this business with the proverb is Socrates' last conversation before his eventual arrival at the party, let us consider it further. The following aspects of it seem odd on consideration:

1. The two bits of Homer that Socrates yokes together are from opposite ends of the *Iliad,* book 2 and book 17.
2. Agamemnon is a great fighter but not much of a general; he caused Achilles' revolt.
3. Menelaus is not a feeble fighter at all but was called that by a god who was *lying* to Paris, persuading him to fight a much more powerful opponent—Menelaus.
4. Homer has an entire epic poem about just this subject, a good man coming unbidden to the feast of bad men: the *Odyssey.*[6]

Why does Socrates come up with this elaborate, artificial, and implausible example of Homer's "ruining" the proverb? Perhaps he is thinking of himself as a kind of Odysseus, returning, however late, to the scene of the Suitors' feast to claim what is rightfully his, namely, knowledge of eros, to which *they* arrogantly pretend but which *he* genuinely possesses: "*ta erotika* is the one thing I understand." This knowledge of eros does turn out to involve his close relationship to a female figure (Diotima, the circumspect Penelope of *Symposium*).

SOCRATES AS AN ODYSSEUS FIGURE: THE SECOND PROVERB

The chat with Aristodemus ends with another (mis)quotation from Homer: "*we two going down the road together* shall plan what to say," Socrates says, meaning that as a pair they will make up an excuse for Aristodemus. The Homeric quotation is the italicized part, whose form here in *Iliad* book 10 is somewhat longer:

However, if some other man would go with me, there would be
More comfort and confident strength. *When two go together,*
One at least can look forward and see the advantage,
Whereas if a man by himself discerns anything,
Still he is likely to hesitate sadly and make
Disastrous mistakes . . .
. . . .
                     . . . Then again
Diomedes spoke out among them: "If you really want me
To choose a companion myself, how could I forget
Godlike Odysseus, whose heart and manly spirit
Are eager and ready beyond the daring of others
When it comes to dangerous toil of any kind—
And Pallas Athena adores him. If he will go with me,
The two of us might go through flaming fire
And come back alive, for no one else can think
So quickly and well."[7]

Here Diomedes has resolved to go on a very dangerous night raid against the Trojan camp, for which he needs to choose a partner. At first his words suggest that, as the proverb is generally translated, "two heads are better than one," but later the sense changes to suggest simply that *Odysseus's* head is better than any other. Again it seems remarkable that this should be the passage that comes to Socrates' mind as he walks to Agathon's dinner party with Aristodemus: a night raid in enemy territory! But if we bear in mind the traditional Platonic rivalry between philosophy and poetry, and the fact that Socrates shied away from the very crowd that granted the victory crown to Agathon, Socrates' apprehension and his martial outlook may seem more understandable.

SOCRATES' EXTRAORDINARY HABIT

So Aristodemus arrives at the party alone, with neither Socrates nor the excuse he was promised. Agathon's courtesy relieves the embarrassment this might have caused, and a slave is sent out to look for Socrates, soon returning to say: "Socrates is here. He's retreated to the neighbor's porch, and is standing there; when I call him, he isn't willing to come in." Agathon replies, "How extraordinary [*atopos*]!" And Aristodemus defends Socrates, saying "It's a way [*ethos*] he has." A little later, halfway through the dinner, Socrates does come in, and Agathon asks him: "Here, Socrates, lie down beside me, so that in touching you I may have the benefit of the wisdom that came to you on the porch. For clearly you found it, and you now possess it, or you wouldn't have moved." (175d)

This is our first experience of Socrates' "extraordinary" (*atopon*) habit of suddenly standing apart in intense concentration.[8] That habit will appear again at 220c, where Alcibiades describes a similar incident in camp on the army's campaign at Potidaea—only that time, Socrates remained lost in thought for an entire day and all the following night. There is an implied similarity between that incident of Socrates' trance and this one: perhaps this banquet of Agathon's, too, is a kind of campaign, to which the semimilitary rhetoric of Socrates' "retreat" to the porch is perfectly appropriate.

Indeed symposia were, like so much of upper-class Athenian life, from the courts and the Assembly to the athletic games and the drama festivals, agonistic: participation was competitive and tended to reproduce the Homeric obsession with that always-scarce resource, honor. These echoes of the *Iliad,* and of the recent Athenian battles like Potidaea, may be designed as whispered reminders to the reader that, beneath the gentleman's courtesy of Agathon and Socrates, there is an *agon* being fought whose stakes are rather higher than they appear. The echoes of the *Odyssey*—for instance, the quotation from book 4 with which Alcibiades introduces the Potidaea story at 220c, "Here's another exploit the indomitable man performed"—suggest that Socrates' reliance on the intellect resembles that of Odysseus: each is a hero of knowledge, who exerts considerable pressure on the values of his contemporaries.

THE WOOL ANALOGY

To return to 175d, Agathon seems to think he can benefit directly from Socrates' weird habit, hoping if not to acquire the habit itself— the ability to concentrate exclusively on a given intellectual problem—

at least to acquire the *product* of the habit, namely, this or that bit of wisdom. This is Agathon's naïveté about knowledge, to which Socrates directs two rejoinders. The first one is uttered on the spot: "Socrates sat down and said, 'It would be very fine indeed, Agathon, if wisdom were that sort of thing, so that if we touched one another it flowed from those of us who were more full with it, into those who were emptier, just as water in drinking cups flows through a strip of wool, from the fuller into the emptier," (175d).

The second rejoinder comes much later: it is the part of Socrates' own speech in which he says how he thinks knowledge *does* work, and it certainly is not as Agathon had pictured it:

> But what is by far even more extraordinary than this, is not just that our knowledges come to be ours, and are lost from us again: even we ourselves are never the same with respect to knowledge, since the very same thing happens to every single bit of what we know. What we call "practice", for instance, exists because knowledge leaks out of us: forgetting is knowledge's going-out.... (208a)

This goes against Agathon's emphasis on the finding and *holding* of knowledge. Just because Socrates made a discovery on the neighbor's front porch (if indeed he did) does not mean he will possess that discovery forever, nor can Agathon imbibe it simply by touching Socrates in the reclining leisure of a drinking party. But it turns out that knowledge is, after all, something that flows, and the wool analogy is not totally without merit. It may even remind us of another bit of science metaphor, the chain of iron rings in the *Ion,* which it curiously resembles. The divine mania of *poetic* inspiration is the kind of thing you *can* transmit from one person to another (at least, from Muse to poet to rhapsode to audience). Socratic reverie on the porch, which is presumably a species of *philosophic* mania, is not so easily transmitted. Once Socrates has "found" whatever he learned in his trancelike state, it is just a normal bit of knowledge, apt to flow away into oblivion, to nobody's especial benefit unless practice replaces it.

Continuing from where we left off at 175d, the wool analogy also has a sexual overtone:

"If wisdom *is* that way, I highly prize [the opportunity] to recline beside you, for I hope to be filled up with abundant and beautiful wisdom from you. For my own wisdom may prove quite insignificant, and debatable, just as a dream is; whereas yours is brilliant, and full of potential, since in spite of your youth, it shone out so brightly and became so manifest the day before yesterday, before the witness of more than 30 thousand of the Greeks."

"You are hubristic [*hubristês ei*], Socrates," said Agathon. "We'll go to legal arbitration a little later, you and I, over the issue of our wisdom, using Dionysus as the judge." (175d–e)

The speeches of Phaedrus and Pausanias are about sexual love for adolescent boys, and though anal intercourse is not the major possible expression of that love, it is an ever-present possibility, so that some of the rhetorical action in those speeches consists in keeping this specific form of sex safely contained inside various cultural parentheses. The Athenian vocabulary for offensive sexual domination is *hubris*, the same term for excessive pride or self-assertion familiar to modern readers of Aristotle's *Poetics*. Agathon's overt purpose in calling Socrates a *hubristês* is to rebuke him for his irony about Agathon's wisdom; his secondary meaning is a response to Socrates' sexual innuendo on its own terms.[9]

The rhetoric of litigation foreshadows the courtroom scene in *Apology,* of which Alcibiades' speech is also a prefiguration (for instance, at 219c5 he addresses the symposiasts as "gentlemen of the jury"). Dionysus is the judge because the Lenaean Festival was in his honor and so, therefore, are yesterday's victory dinner and today's symposium. But Dionysus is not only the god of theater but also of wine, and when Socrates drinks everyone else under the table we can take it that Dionysus has judged in his favor and not Agathon's, after all.

THE PROPOSAL FOR SPEECHES ON EROS

At 176a the dining part of the symposium is concluded, the religious rites are performed, and the question of the night's drinking is broached at last. Everyone agrees that after the excesses of the previous night, tonight's consumption of wine should be more conservative and up to each man to decide for himself. At some symposia, the "master of the symposium" directs the drinking, and refusals on the part of the other guests are considered bad form. Tonight no one will have that to worry about. Eryximachus the doctor gives some rather stodgy advice about the bad health brought on by too much wine; then he dismisses the flute-girl; and finally, he proposes that they spend the night in conversation.

At this point Eryximachus quotes Euripides' (now lost) play *Melanippe,* saying that the proposal is " 'not my own tale, but it comes from—' Phaedrus." This echoes the very beginning of *Symposium,* where Apollodorus urges that he is not telling his own story but one he heard from Aristodemus. It also anticipates the end of the dialogue, where Socrates apparently tells Diotima's story rather than improvise one of his own. Eryximachus explains that Phaedrus has often complained to him that while the poets have made hymns and paeans of praise to practically every other god, they have neglected Eros. "One smart man even wrote a book which praises Salt ... while to this day, no one has dared worthily to praise Eros." So Eryximachus proposes that they each make such a speech in praise of Eros, beginning with Phaedrus, since he is "the father of the discussion."

4

The Speech of Phaedrus: Praise and Blame

Paiderasty

Paiderasty (from *pais* [boy] + *eros*) was a highly conventionalized erotic relationship between men and adolescent boys. It seems to have been a regular part of Athenian life partly because women's lives were more or less strictly segregated from those of men, and this diminished both the opportunity and the incentive for forming satisfying heterosexual relationships. Whatever the many causes, there was a largely aristocratic subculture of paiderasty in Athens, and much of the speeches of Phaedrus and especially Pausanias are devoted to spelling out its conventions. These amount to an elastic moral calculus within which participants could explain their behavior to themselves, to their lovers, and, not least, to the various persons attached to whichever partner was the younger, including fathers, brothers, tutors, and guardians.[1]

The one who pursues—generally but not always the older partner—is called the *erastês* (plural *erastai*), or "lover," and the pursued, generally a teenager, is the *eromenos* (plural *eromenoi*), a passive participle meaning "loved one" (another common term is *paidika* [boy]).

In sympathetic accounts, this relationship is considered a benefit to both partners, so long as both possess "virtue"; and the ideal version of such a relationship is imagined as the equal exchange of the erastês's wisdom for the eromenos's sexual favors. These are treated euphemistically in *Symposium*, though Attic comedy (especially Aristophanes) is quite explicit about them. Only the role of the passive partner in anal intercourse seems to have been held in contempt; the active role was apparently not looked down upon. It seems to be the case, from vase paintings and other evidence, that an erastês could be expected to fondle the genitals of his eromenos as a greeting—but the eromenos was expected to be coy, remain unaroused, and in general to deny that this aspect of the relationship especially interested him. To do otherwise would be to risk a permanent identification with the sexually passive role, in short, to be "made into a woman"—whereas the proper business of an adolescent male is to emulate the masculine ethos of citizenship, which is active and dominant.[2]

THE FIRST SPEECH: EROS IS THE FIRST GOD

Phaedrus is a young man at this point, enamored with the charismatic effects of rhetoric. In the Platonic dialogue that bears his name, a kind of sister-dialogue to *Symposium*, he walks with Socrates in the countryside and reads aloud a speech of his favorite author, the professional rhetorician Lysias. Socrates and Phaedrus appear there as potential lovers but politely refer to themselves as "lovers of discourse," which they certainly are. In *Symposium* Phaedrus has become "the father of the discourse," and we should note the language of procreation in both phrases, since several speakers (e.g., Pausanias and Diotima) compare male intellectual fertility to female birth-giving.

We can guess that Eryximachus was put up to his proposal by Phaedrus (that would certainly make Phaedrus the father of the discourse), who has a wonderful opportunity to test his skill and to learn from the performances of his elders. His host, Agathon, shares Phaedrus's addiction to rhetoric, but whereas Phaedrus imitates Lysias—

the relatively sober and pragmatic rhetorician whose hired speeches got many wealthy Athenians out of their legal troubles—Agathon is a fan of Gorgias of Leontini, whose elaborately embellished style was superb for dazzling large crowds but was often nearly useless for thinking. At 175e Socrates calls Agathon's wisdom "*lampros* [shining, brilliant] and full of potential." *Brilliant* is also the meaning of Phaedrus's name, and both of these speakers fall victim to the aestheticism that made the art of rhetoric dangerous: it spins out shiny surfaces, distracting hearers and speakers alike from the underlying truth or falsehood of what is said.

Phaedrus's speech is a standard encomium, or praise speech, a genre that focuses first on the noble lineage of the one being praised, and then on the benefits he bestows. The points he makes are these:

1. Eros is a primordial god. He has no parents, and the poet Hesiod says he came into being very early, preceded only by Chaos and Earth; the philosopher Parmenides says Eros is the eldest.
2. Being eldest, he bestows the greatest benefits; namely,
3. the relationships of erastês and eromenos, or rather the chief benefit instilled by their love, namely,
4. shame over what is ugly, and ambition (literally, love of honor) for what is beautiful.
5. More than anyone else's, a lover's watch over our behavior intensifies the shame we feel on shameful occasions; therefore
6. an army made up entirely of lovers would be invincible: on the one hand, because anyone would rather die than feel such shame; on the other, because love inspires great courage,
7. even the courage to die for one another (whether male or female), which is exemplified in the Alcestis story (a familiar myth that Phaedrus summarizes)
8. but not in the story of Orpheus, since Orpheus merely went down to Hades alive;
9. whereas Achilles, in the *Iliad,* died for his erastês Patroclus, even after Patroclus was already dead; which is why
10. Aeschylus was wrong in saying that Achilles was the erastês of Patroclus, since Achilles was by far the more beautiful one and was much younger.

11. The gods are more amazed and impressed when an eromenos loves his erastês than the reverse, since the erastês is more divine, being filled with the god (Eros); that is why the gods rewarded Achilles with an afterlife on the Isles of the Blessed.[3]

"Phaedrus made some speech of such a sort as that," as the narration says. As we read the speech, its logic seems rather loose-knit: point 9 comes out of the blue, until point 10 relates it to point 8. This is a bit awkward, since points 8 and 10 both claim to be causal explanations for Achilles' reward on the Isles of the Blessed, itself a lengthy phrase that Phaedrus gives twice. But apart from these rather technical concerns, there is a troubling ethical issue pervading the whole speech: praise and blame are, indeed, deeply traditional motives for behavior in classical Athens, but the public economy of shame is supposed to be more important than the private one. The political ideal of Athenian public life (as described, say, in Pericles' Funeral Oration—where the citizens are urged to become "Athens' lovers") expects that the polis itself provides sufficient emotional incentive for zealous right conduct. Phaedrus's suggestion, that to include only pairs of lovers and beloveds would be the best way to organize "a polis or an army," reminds us of this public ideal by presupposing its weakness and failure. After all, if our political culture is in good order, you do not need to be my lover to inhibit my doing something shameful; our shared devotion to the city is deterrent enough.

From the Socratic point of view, the problem lies with praise and blame themselves, not with their source. The fear of disgrace and the lust for honor are merely extrinsic and superficial motivations for human conduct. In fact, praise and blame are to the Good as Rhetoric is to Philosophy. This will emerge again at 194a, when Socrates and Agathon wrangle about the importance of praise from the many, compared with praise from the few (a discussion that echoes the contrast between last night's big victory celebration and tonight's intimate symposium).

Before we leave Phaedrus, let us take a closer look at point 7, the denunciation of Orpheus. What precedes it is the praise of Alcestis (whose story can be read in Euripides' play that bears her name). She alone was willing to die in her husband's stead, and the gods were so impressed by her deed that they let her soul out of Hades.

> But Orpheus the son of Oeagrus they sent out from Hades with his goal unaccomplished, having shown him the phantom of his wife, for whom he had come there, but not giving her to him, because he seemed to them to be soft; since, after all, he was a musician, and because he did not dare to die on behalf of his love, as Alcestis did, but devised a way to go into Hades while still living. Accordingly they punished him, and they caused his death to occur at the hands of women; not like Achilles the son of Thetis, whom they honored and sent into the Isles of the Blessed.... (179d–e)

The disdain for musicians is conventional, but note the term "to be *soft*" (*malthakizesthai*). It will come up again in both Pausanias and Agathon. The figure being contrasted with Achilles here is Orpheus, who went down to Hades while still alive—as did Odysseus. Later, at the conclusion of the speech of Agathon, Socrates will quote a passage from *Odyssey* book 10 in which Odysseus leaves Hades for fear of the monstrous Gorgon-head (whose gaze turns people to stone). Agathon has just finished delivering a speech in the ornate style of the rhetorician Gorgias, and the point of Socrates' joke is the pun on his name (Gorgias = Gorgon), with its implicit comparison between the dazzling rhetorical effects of the one and the petrifying gaze of the other. Most of the speakers seem to identify themselves primarily as participants in erotic relationship, and when Socrates claims "the erotic is the one thing I understand," he appears to do the same. But his speech is an effort to redefine the seeker of knowledge as a special (indeed, the fundamental) kind of lover; that is, to include among the lovers a philosopher whose only true interest is in knowledge and not in what we normally think of as human relationship. This is why Phaedrus dwells on the *katabasis* (journey to Hades) of various lovers, while Socrates invokes that of Odysseus, the seeker of knowledge.

As Stanley Rosen has explained, Phaedrus's continual focus upon the well-being of the beloved—even to the point of making the gods themselves into the "amazed" onlookers, and rewarders, of the beloved—springs from selfishness (and amounts to a kind of hubris) (Rosen, 50–59). Phaedrus is, apparently, the eromenos of Eryximachus,[4] and his absorption in the beloved's position is such that he omits any serious reference to the fates of the lovers in his examples. He prefers Alcestis to Orpheus because she glorified the beloved more, by making a greater sacrifice; as for the lover's well-being, Phaedrus is quite dismissive of it. Rosen makes the incisive point that Phaedrus alone, of all the speakers, is unconcerned with any kind of generativity, whether biological or mental, and this follows from his concern to deny that Eros has any parents. In consequence, each of his three anecdotes ends with the deaths of both partners; only Alcestis is redeemed from death, though not from mortality—she is denied the reward Phaedrus grants to Achilles, since she is only a lover whereas Achilles was a beloved (like Phaedrus). The emphasis on reward in the last lines of his speech is consistent with the earlier emphasis on praise and blame.

5

The Speech of Pausanias:
A Sophisticated Relativism

Intervening Speeches Lost

There were some other speeches between those of Phaedrus and Pausanias, but Aristodemus could not remember them, and so we know nothing of them—neither the speeches themselves nor the speakers. A few centuries after Plato, the Roman poet Horace wrote, "Many heroes lived before Agamemnon; but all are overwhelmed in unending night, unwept, unknown, because they lack a sacred bard" (Ode IV). Plato did not have to write our line at 180c about the lost intervening speeches, and his having done so is another instance of his vivid awareness of *writing* as the medium of that fame for which his contemporaries, and his ancestors, were always competing. Homer saved Agamemnon from oblivion, but he was (we now believe) an oral poet, and it is the bard, not the scribe, who first performs this immortalizing work on the heroes' behalf. But the bards had their day, and with the advent of writing and literacy the oral performance becomes the preserve of a professionalized class of nonimprovising reciters, or "rhapsodes."[1] Writing becomes the way the business of culture is done, and without it the revolution brought about by Sophistical rhetoric would have been impossible.

In Plato this issue takes on a new force, because whereas Socrates wrote nothing, Plato is a consummate writer. The bold and extemporaneous dialectic to which Socrates was so thoroughly committed led to his execution by the state in 399 B.C.E., a moment when Athenian glory—military, civic, and literary—was in headlong decline. Conditions had so deteriorated that, in Athens at least, it would probably have been both imprudent and ineffective for Plato to emulate Socrates and converse rather than compose. But this was no arbitrary choice; at 275a Socrates states his suspicion that books create a mere illusion of wisdom in their readers, who yet lack the chastening experience of spontaneous dialectic. In becoming a writer, Plato had to overcome, or at least resist, this and other dangers inherent in the written word. This is a major element of our understanding of why he wrote dialogues, rather than treatises: unlike the treatises of, say, Aristotle, the Platonic dialogue holds competing positions in tension, avoiding the illusion that an authoritative truth can be transmitted, much less created, without long dialectical labor.

Like Apollodorus's admission (178a) that he only remembered the majority of what Aristodemus told him, the mention of forgotten speeches at 180c reminds us of the limitations of a strictly oral economy of information. It makes us more sympathetic to Plato's break with the Socratic prejudice against the written word, and by reminding us that we are reading a text it sharpens our attention to the differences between Plato's writings and those of the Sophists.

PAUSANIAS'S CLEVER PAIDERASTY

The Sophistry to which Phaedrus aspires, Pausanias has achieved, and his courtroom tone is the result of a successful tutelage in rhetorical improvisation. At the beginning of his speech Phaedrus praised "the great Prodicus," a popular Sophist and probably the teacher of both Pausanias and Agathon (see *Protagoras* 315c). Prodicus was noted for two things especially: his cleverness at drawing fine distinctions in the meanings of near synonyms (an achievement matched by the modern philosopher J. L. Austin), and an equally clever epigram on love: "Desire doubled is Eros; Eros doubled is madness."[2] Pausanias imitates Prodicus in both of these, since he distinguishes the base Eros from the noble Eros and, in so doing, doubles Eros.

THE DOUBLE EROS

Pausanias begins with the statement that Eros is double, not unitary, and therefore it is necessary to distinguish which Eros is deserving of praise and to eulogize only that Eros. Here is the next length of Pausanias's argument, broken down into a list, with some of the important Greek terms transliterated and then defined in brackets:

1. There is no Aphrodite without Eros; if the former were unitary, so would the latter be;
2. but as it is, Aphrodite is double, and so therefore is Eros.
3. The older Aphrodite we call Uranian; she is the daughter of *Uranos* [Heaven]; she has no mother. The younger Aphrodite, daughter of Zeus and Dione, we call *Pandemic* [common, vulgar; literally "of all the people"].
4. Each Eros must share the name of the Aphrodite with whom he does his work.
5. All gods deserve our praise, but their domains must be distinguished, each to each;
6. "for all *praxis* [action] is such, that in itself it is neither *kalos* [noble, beautiful] nor *aischros* [shameful, ugly] ... each turns out to be the sort it is in the doing, as it is done, noble if done nobly, base if basely; and so it is with Eros." (180e–181a; 183d)
6A. Pandemic Eros, being by far the younger, and partaking of both male and female,
    a. works *hoti an tuchê* [by chance, at random, haphazardly] (181b);
    b. and in *hoi phauloi* [(people who are) of no account, insignificant, petty];
    c. they love women as well as boys;

    d. they love bodies more than (or, "rather than") souls; since

    e. they love the most mindless ones they can find,

    f. looking only to the satisfaction of their goal,[3] careless whether it is done nobly or not; hence, whatever they can get away with, that they do;

6B.   but the other Eros is from Uranian Aphrodite, who partakes of male only, being older, and having no part in *hubris* [brutality, insolence, vulgarity]; this is the love for boys (181c4);

    a. those who are *epipnoi* [inspired] by this Eros turn, loving, to the male, which is by nature the stronger and the one with more mind;

    b. you can recognize, in paiderasty itself, those moved purely by this Eros: they love boys only when the boys have begun to be strong in mind: when their beards are beginning to grow. (181d)

Before we go any further down Pausanias's line of reasoning, let us take stock of its course hitherto. Point 5 is, as Dover indicates, "a verbal gesture to avoid Nemesis [the punishment the gods inflict on those who speak impiously]; Pausanias does not in fact find anything to commend in Eros Pandemos" (1980, 97). This suggests that the speech's claims to piety are a self-serving disguise for a tissue of argumentation in behalf of Pausanias's own erotic tastes.

    Note the way the genealogies of the gods, including this double genealogy of Aphrodite, preserve the connection between the authority of the gods and their primordiality. We can see this in the noun *archê*, which means "rule, dominion" as well as "beginning." Both Pausanias and Phaedrus rightly take for granted this traditional nexus of the early and the powerful, in phrases like "being the eldest he confers the greatest benefits" (178c) and "the older Aphrodite we call Heavenly" (180d). But as the speech proceeds, Pausanias seems to reduce the gods to a superfluous rubric under which each kind of person does whatever it is in his nature to do.

    Point 6 is a cardinal aspect of the relativism that Pausanias's talk about the god is designed to conceal. It is the dark side of the incomplete self-knowledge to which the Sophists and their students attained, and after many centuries of oblivion it reemerges in the soul-searching of the late Renaissance and the Reformation. Hamlet says it on the stage: "there is nothing either good or bad but thinking makes it so," a few years after Martin Luther says it from the pulpit: "As the man is, whether believer or unbeliever, so also is his work—good if it was done in faith, wicked if it was done in unbelief."[4] From the Socratic point of view, some such relativism is (potentially) the beginning of wisdom, an exit from the darkness of a decaying tradition and into the light of philosophy, by which that tradition might be renewed. But what follows Pausanias's declaration in point 6 is not quite philosophical. So far he has merely reduced love to two categories, a good and a bad, and then ascribed a list of characteristics to each. These characteristics amount to criteria for deciding "how it is done," that is, they enable us to enter the relativism of point 6 armed with a shared schema for evaluating the "how" in question. The trouble comes when the reasons adduced in support of these criteria begin to contradict one another. To continue:

7. "Those who begin to love them at that point (when the beard begins) are prepared to spend their lives in common, loving for their whole lives, rather than deceiving them, and taking them in the imprudence of their youth, and then jeering as they leave, and turning to another."

8. "There ought to be a law against loving *young* boys—to prevent all that serious effort being spent on a matter whose outcome is uncertain: for it's not at all clear at what level of virtue or badness, in soul or body, the outcome [the maturity] of young boys will eventuate."

9. "Good men make this law for themselves anyway, but those who don't, the Pandemic lovers, must be constrained, as we try to constrain them not to love freeborn women; it's these lovers who have brought about the reproach by which some people dare to say that it's a shameful thing to gratify a lover!"

10. "They say this with such cases in view, seeing how inopportune and unjust *those* lovers' actions are; since surely, if those actions—any actions whatever—were done in an orderly way and in accordance with *nomos* ['law' or 'custom'], they wouldn't justly bear reproach." (181d–182a6)

It turns out (in point 8) that the reason one should not love boys younger than the age of incipient wisdom (that is, late puberty, "when the beard starts to grow") is that one's effort might be wasted. The paiderast's fear of wasted effort is usually focused on the prospect of fighting a long erotic agon with a boy and never winning it by getting any sexual favors; here, however, in the Uranian noble paiderasty, the "wasted effort" to be feared is simply that of loving a boy who, like all prepubescents, might or might not turn out to be virtuous in body and soul. That would be a waste indeed, since enlightened Uranian Eros can only be fulfilling if both partners are virtuous. But if this is the reason for a law against loving young boys—to save the erastês from wasting his effort—then that law cannot really be compared with the law against loving unmarried freeborn women, as it is in point 9. The rationale for the statutes protecting the chastity of women was certainly not to prevent male seekers of extramarital sex from wasting their effort; it was first of all to secure the rights of the men legitimately connected with the women in question (fathers, brothers, and husbands) and, in some apparently secondary way, to protect the women themselves from the "ruination" that unsanctioned female sexual activity entailed. We see at 183c–d that Pausanias is unconcerned about the interests of those men:

> But since fathers put chaperones in charge of the eromenoi lest they be allowed to converse with the erastai (and these are the orders given to the chaperone concerning the matter), and the boys of [an eromenos's] own age, and his companions, reproach him if they see this sort of thing occur; and elders neither prevent them reproaching him, nor upbraid the reproachers for speaking improperly—because of this, an observer might well believe that this sort of thing [that is, gratifying a paiderastic lover] is here [that is, in Athens] held to be most disgraceful. But I think it's like this: it is no simple matter, but one which (from the beginning) was said to be neither noble, nor, in its own right, base, but noble if done nobly, and base if basely. (183c4–d6)

These nervous fathers, tutors, and guardians must simply be afraid that the lover is Pandemic and so likely to leave the boy after conquering him. Presumably, if all lovers were Uranian paiderasts, faithful and steadfast, interested more in the soul than in the body, and having "no share in the female," fathers and tutors would have no reason to drive them away. But then, there would soon be no more youths to seduce, since the Uranian Eros, however fertile in soul it may be, is not fertile in body.

Note that when Pausanias reminds us that paiderasty "was said from the beginning to be neither noble nor base," the phrase "from the beginning" (*ex archês*) refers primarily to the beginning of his own speech, but since this speech is precisely about the relativism of paiderasty's detractors as against the divine roots of its legitimacy, he probably also intends a mythological claim in the same phrase, "from the beginning."

As Phaedrus the eromenos made his account favor the interests of eromenoi, Pausanias the erastês favors the interests of those who play *his* role. Within that group, he holds some in contempt and elevates others, and while he claims to base that division on the virtuous and the shameful, his real criteria turn out to be matters of style or, to use the word most appropriate to the Sophistry of the speech—technique.

> 11. "In other cities the laws about paiderasty are more or less easy to understand, for they are defined simply; but here [in Athens] and in Sparta, they are intricate. In Elis and Boeotia, and wherever else people are not articulate, it has been quite simply set up as law, that to gratify lovers is noble; and no one young or old would call it shameful. I think they've done this [that is, made the simple law] in order not to have the ordeal of persuading the boys, since they're incompetent at arguing." (182a7–b7)

This is dubious because Sparta, too, had a reputation for a striking lack of eloquence (as well as plenty of paiderasty); and because the youth or age of the eromenoi is what is in question, not that of the critics; and because the cynical hypothesis about the reason for the law (namely, that it saves the tongue-tied Boeotians from having to seduce their beloveds using an eloquence they do not have) begs the question of the possible ethical warrant for the law. The possibility of that ethical warrant was what brought up the subject of other cities and their diverse nomoi, but now it has disappeared.

12. "But in Ionia and many other places where they live under the power of the barbarians, it is held by *nomos* to be shameful. For the barbarians hold this thing, along with the love of wisdom [*philosophia*] and the love of naked exercise [*philogymnastia*], to be disgraceful, on account of their own tyranny; since, I think, it doesn't benefit the rulers for high thoughts to be engendered among the ruled, nor that the ruled should have strong loyalties in common: which these things, especially Eros, certainly tend to instill."

13. "Tyrants of this land [Athens] learned this by experience: for the love of Aristogeiton and Harmodius grew to be so steadfast that it dissolved their [the tyrants'] rule."

14. "Thus, wherever it is held shameful to gratify a lover, that outlook is due to the evil of those who set up such a standard; that is, to the greedy presumption of the rulers, and to the unmanliness [that is, cowardice] of the ruled."

15. "And where it is simply legislated that lover-gratifying is noble, this is due to a certain laziness of soul in the legislators."

16. "The *nomoi* that have been set up in this country are better by far than these, and as I said, they're not easily understood. Consider that we call it better to love openly than in secret, and especially if the lovers are among the great and the most noble—even if perhaps less beautiful than others are." (182b7–d7)

Rosen has pointed out that this concern with ugliness (loving the uglier man is better) is a personal touch from Pausanias; it may be ironic self-mockery, uttered with a smile, but it does figure in the argument, where it is simply self-serving. A wholesale cultural-legislative acceptance of lover-gratifying would usher in a flood of competition from lovers who lack Pausanias's eloquence (and ugliness), whereas an equally general condemnation of it would condemn Pausanias along with the Pandemic lovers he despises. The trick is to construct an account of Eros that is, like the Athenian *nomos* according to Pausanias, sufficiently "complex" to favor those lovers most like Pausanias: those who are clever speakers (that is, learned in such rhetoric as this speech demonstrates), older, uglier, and committed to a single partner.

17. "A lover receives amazing encouragement from all sides, not at all as if he were doing something shameful: but when he has conquered, that seems to be honorable, and when he hasn't, shameful."

18. "And concerning the struggle to succeed, the *nomos* permits the lover to be praised who does shocking things—things which, if someone dared to do them in any other pursuit, desiring to bring about any accomplishment other than this one [that is, erotic success], he would reap the greatest reproaches ... begging and pleading in prayer, swearing oaths, sleeping in doorways, and generally slaving away as no slave would willingly do ... strangest of all, as the common multitude [*hoi polloi*] say, is that the gods permit perjury only in the case of lovers' oaths, since an oath of Aphrodite is no oath at all." (182d7–183b7, with omissions)

Here Pausanias makes the point quoted above, about fathers and tutors; he then repeats points 6 and 7, and then his argument continues:

19. "Our [Athenian] *nomos* provides an excellent and proper test for distinguishing the two sorts of lovers [Pandemic, fleeting lovers of the body, which withers, versus Uranian, faithful lovers of the soul, which endures], by encouraging the ermenoi to flee the one kind and gratify the other. This is why it [*nomos*] encourages lovers to pursue and beloveds to run away. It makes for a struggle and a test, as to which kind of lover is there, and which kind of beloved. And this is also why it is considered shameful to prevail right away." (184a1–a6)

20. The next section of the speech is a lengthy formulation of the following idea: just as it was acceptable for the lover to be a slave in wooing the beloved, it is also acceptable to be a slave to somebody who confers education and improvement in return for this willing slavery.

Point 17 claims that success and failure are the salient criteria of praiseworthiness and shamefulness, and Pausanias never really integrates those criteria into the others he develops at greater pains and in greater detail. He makes point 17, about success and failure, in order to make the slavery of the lover in point 18 seem as though it is at least partially directed toward the winning of *praise*, that ancient and hallowed object of desire, rather than purely for sexual favors, which would be a base (indeed, a pandemic) goal. And yet it is precisely to the multitude (*pan* [entire] +: *demos* [the people]) that Pausanias appeals for the starkly hubristic right to swear false oaths in the name of Eros.

LIKE SUPERIOR KNOWLEDGE, SUPERIOR LOVE HAS AN ABIDING OBJECT

Note that in point 19, Pausanias points to a match between lovers and the way they love. A Uranian, steadfast lover directs his affection primarily toward the soul of his beloved, because the soul is, like Uranian love, steadfast and enduring. But a Pandemic lover is as ephemeral as the bodily beauty to which his love is directed: "he is inconstant because the thing he loves is inconstant" (183e). This resembles the account of knowledge that Diotima will unfold in the speech of Socrates. In that account, the philosopher finds the most worthy object of love not among bodies or even among beautiful souls but beyond these in a vision of the eternal Beauty, "the beautiful itself unto itself." Later on, Diotima speaks of contemplating this ultimate Beauty "with that which *can* contemplate it" (212a), namely, the intellect, a faculty of the soul. This kinship between the soul and the object of its knowledge (both of which are immaterial and enduring) is rather like Pausanias's match between the enduring, Uranian love and its enduring object (183e).

EVEN EXCHANGE

Now there follows the climax of Pausanias's whole speech, the working up of the conventional wisdom about paiderasty: that it amounts to an even exchange, of the wisdom of the erastês for the sexual favors of the eromenos:

> For when lover [*erastes*] and beloved [*paidika*] come together—
> each guided by his own *nomos*: the former, of serving (in what-
> ever way he may justly serve) the beloved who has gratified him;
> the latter, of serving (in whatever way he may justly serve) this
> man who is making him wise and good; and the lover, being
> capable of it [*dunamenos*], contributes intelligence and the
> remainder of the virtues, and the beloved, needing [*deomenos*] to
> acquire education and the remainder of wisdom—then indeed,
> these separate *nomoi* coincide, into a single, self-same *nomos*;
> and only there and nowhere else can it occur, that a beloved can
> honorably indulge his lover. (184d3–e4)

This is the conventional model on which Socrates and Agathon base
their banter at 175e. It also forms the expectations that Alcibiades
brings to his attempted seduction of Socrates (216–219). Pausanias
employs the participle *deomenos* (needing, being in need) for the
beloved's neediness with respect to education. This is cognate with
Alcibiades' own phrase, *endeôs ôn*, (being in need [216a5]) for those
personal deficiencies that philosophical dialogue, and the consequent
self-scrutiny, have brought to his attention. It is striking that Pausanias's conventional model of paiderasty prescribes an erotic agon with
a virtuous lover as just the right supply for what is lacking in such a
youth, and that Alcibiades tried to take this avenue, only to be rejected
by his chosen lover Socrates. This happened because Socrates' version
of philosophy does indeed confer the very virtues Alcibiades lacks, but
without demanding the reciprocation of sexual favors; whereas Alcibiades not only wants to be seduced by Socrates (and he admits that this
effectively reverses the roles, making Alcibiades himself the seducer),
he also lacks the patience for a chaste philosophical education. It
seems that Pausanias, for all his self-serving casuistry, starts from the
premise that human beings have erotic needs, and then constructs a
model of erotic relationship by which those erotic needs (for sexual
gratification), as well as other needs that might best be called
metaerotic (since for Pausanias, "intelligence and the rest of virtue . . .
education and the rest of wisdom," are functions of eros), can be met.

6

The Speech of Eryximachus:
Medicine and Love

THE HICCUPS

Aristophanes would have spoken next, we are told, but he had an attack of the hiccups. So he turned to Eryximachus, the doctor, and said "you're the right person either to stop these hiccups of mine, or to speak in my stead until they go away." These are perhaps the most famous hiccups in Western literature (that is, much ink has been spilled over their possible meanings) and they are worth some interpretive consideration.

The comedies of Aristophanes are replete with bodily functions, and while these are often funny in their own right, the sneezes and farts also form a parody of heroic individualism, as well as a revision of it in humbler terms. The desires of the Aristophanic hero are largely bodily demands (for instance, good food, sex, and a comfortable bed), not so grand as those of the Homeric hero for fame or the tragic hero for justice, but in Aristophanes these more realistic desires take hold of the audience with a powerful, if comic, effect because they are so much more common as genuine desires. What is uncommon is the courage and stature with which the Aristophanic hero pursues what he so humbly wants, and when we come to Aristophanes' speech we will see this strange combination of greatness and embodiment in new terms.

The Eros whom the symposiasts have set out to praise is indeed a god, but we can understand his nature not only by remembering the received myths about him but also by considering the way love works, since that is his domain. Where Pausanias examines the workings of love as interpersonal relationship, Eryximachus speaks in the idiom of pre-Socratic philosophy, and treats eros as a cosmological principle or natural force, rather like Strife and Love [*Philia*] in the pre-Socratic philosopher Empedocles. Later, in Socrates' speech, Diotima will combine these two approaches and discuss human eros as the principle of access to an ultimate knowledge of the world's real nature.

Eryximachus's speech is brief, and we can paraphrase it clearly:

1. Pausanias's distinction between a good Uranian Eros and a bad Pandemic Eros makes sense to Eryximachus, but thereafter Pausanias's speech went awry and so the doctor must fix it.

2. Love's sphere of activity is greater than the domain of human bodies and their relations; Love operates in all things, badly in some and well in others, according to the kind of Love involved.

3. As Pausanias claimed it was right to gratify a good lover and wrong to gratify a bad one, so the physician gratifies the healthy parts of the body and denies the ill parts.

4. This gratifying and denying amounts to *filling and emptying* the appropriate parts of the body, so that extremes (e.g., those of heat and cold, moisture and dryness) can be reconciled. Medicine is the addition of the right Love and the subtraction of the wrong one.

5. Eryximachus invokes Heraclitus, and takes issue with him.

6. The difference between the good Uranian Eros and the bad Pandemic Eros comes down to a difference in quantity of appetite: the good is moderate, the bad excessive (Eryximachus gives an example from the balances and imbalances involved in the action of the weather).

7. Religious piety, too, is based on the heeding of the appropriate (moderate) Eros, and divination, which informs us of our religious duties, must also be a kind of regulation of love.

In his zeal to reduce the ethical question—what is Love—to a technical one, Eryximachus nearly loses sight of the question altogether. He extends the sphere of Eros out so far (making it a cosmological principle) that the familiar meaning of love is generalized out of the picture. Among the consequences of this magnifying of Eros is the eclipse of all the other gods. Despite his respectful effort to bring them in at the end, Eryximachus would seem to have replaced Zeus and Apollo and the Furies with a single governing principle, Eros; or rather with two divergent forms of a single Eros, one extreme and the other moderate. If moderation is the *telos,* the thing toward which the doctor aims, we may well wonder whether this is the sort of argumentation that is likely to achieve it.

Before we move on from Eryximachus, let us examine further his little struggle with Heraclitus. It seems as though the purpose of this allusion is to partake of the glory of a revered sage, dignifying the art of medicine by association. But Eryximachus introduces his quotation from the master with the insolent complaint that "Heraclitus didn't express himself eloquently in this particular utterance: 'Unity coheres by divergence within itself, like the harmony of the bow and of the lyre.' "[1] But Heraclitus's remark (the following is Charles Kahn's rendering of it) really begins like this: "*They do not comprehend* how a thing agrees at variance with itself: it is an attunement turning back on itself, like that of the bow and the lyre."[2] So where Eryximachus begins with a complaint that Heraclitus cannot have meant what he said—the words of Heraclitus must be confused, since that would explain how they really say what Eryximachus wants to hear—the actual fragment (as we have it, at least) shows the philosopher complaining of exactly the kind of incomprehension we see here in our good doctor.

Plato, for his part, knew how formidable Heraclitus was and seems to have agreed with his great predecessor in the main question of what the cosmos is like; namely, continual flux with only local and apparent stabilities. But Plato parted company with Heraclitus when he posited an eternal domain of Forms, entirely exempt from the flux that so thoroughly pervades the world of experience. Diotima's speech is a stage in this central development of Plato's thought, and so this part of *Symposium*—in which Eryximachus quotes Heraclitus with a mixture of reverence and insolence—seems to be a piece of Plato's consummate intellectual diplomacy: he hints at Heraclitus's limitations, he gestures toward Heraclitus's unfathomable depths, and he shows how easy it is to blame Heraclitus for one's own incomprehension.

To be fair, Plato later says some very beautiful things in the mouth of Eryximachus—including the formulation that was sufficiently dear to the American poet Hart Crane that he made it the epigraph to his "Atlantis," one of the finest lyrics of modern times: "Music is then the knowledge of that which relates to love in harmony and system." And yet this Eryximachean remark, like those about Love in the weather, or Love in astronomy, only has such poetic power as we bring to it, so that on Crane's page we hear Plato's genius in those words, but when they occur amid the speech of Eryximachus, we may well hear only a pretentious crank whose notion of "Eros" amounts to little more than a sterile puzzle about opposites and categories. Eryximachus is the representative of rationalism and technique, and just as rhetoric failed Phaedrus and ethics failed Pausanias, so medicine proves inadequate for the sense-making task to which Eryximachus puts it here. As *Symposium* proceeds we get the sense that only Poetry (i.e., Agathon the tragedian and Aristophanes the comedian) and Philosophy (Socrates) stand a real chance of success in the task of adequately praising Eros, and the dialogue's uttermost, final page amounts to a verdict.

7

The Speech of Aristophanes:
The Yearning for Wholeness

The transition from Eryximachus to Aristophanes takes the form of Aristophanes' announcement that his hiccups have stopped. He attributes the relief to the doctor's advice, but his tone is half-mocking ("I used the sneezing technique ... the sneezing technique"). Then he begins his speech with a remark about method: "I have in mind to speak in a different way than you and Pausanias." Whatever Eros is, it cannot be fully reducible to the sort of impersonal principle of medical change that Eryximachus makes of it; nor can Pausanias's self-justifying, paiderastic Sophistry be the whole story of Eros. Although each speaker seems to take up and employ elements of the preceding speeches, there are several major changes of approach as *Symposium* unfolds, and we have arrived at one of them here. Aristophanes will go beyond the limitations of his predecessors' uses of *logos* (argument) by appealing to *mythos*.

Myth means story, and the story Aristophanes tells is of human origins. There were originally three sexes, male, female, and androgyn (a combination of the two). People originally were double-bodied, and each individual looked essentially like a couple making love—what

Shakespeare called "the beast with two backs"—except that each of the two faces looked outward toward the world, not inward toward the other half. These double beings, called "the circle-people" in the Platonic commentaries, moved around by turning gymnastic cartwheels on their eight limbs; they were prodigiously fast and strong, *precisely because all their erotic needs were at all times fulfilled.* Their strength and speed led to arrogance: they mounted up to heaven to attack the gods (hence Aristophanes' claim that Homer's myth of the hubristic giants Ephialtes and Otus is really about the circle-people). In response, the gods chose not to destroy mankind, since that would deprive the gods of their sacrifices and honors, but instead to cut them each in half: that way, human beings would be debilitated and humbled, and there would be twice as many of them around to venerate the gods. Zeus himself cut the circle-people in half, and told Apollo to heal them and take up the slack skin into a knot at what became the navel. At this point it became necessary to twist the face around to what is now the front of the body, so that each human being would be able to see the trace of his or her surgical wound (namely, the navel) and be humbled by the memory of failed rebellion.

This remedy was almost adequate, but the poor human beings became so despondent in their new separateness that they began to die out. Here Zeus made a new solution (sexual union) to the problem, completing the first solution (surgical division): he moved their genitals to the front of their bodies and thereby invented human sexual intercourse. Before then, the complete circle-people had only had intercourse "with the ground, like cicadas." So sexual union, which was already, we can assume, the prerogative of the gods, became a central part of the human estate. When Zeus moved the genitals of men around to the front, he saved mankind by restoring our capacity to procreate new individuals and by relieving the longing and melancholy brought on by Apollo's surgery (he also thereby saved the gods, who need the devotion of mankind). With heterosexual procreation the species is preserved, and with homosexual satisfaction achieved, men can "turn to deeds, and pay attention to the other affairs of life." But there is more to Eros than this. Describing the persons fortunate enough to meet their own original "other half," Aristophanes says:

These are the ones who spend their whole lives together, but they can't explain what it is they hope to gain for themselves by being together with one another. For no one would think that it's sex, as if sex were the thing for the sake of which each one accompanies the other and gratifies him thus, with such great zeal. But the soul of each one is clearly desiring something else, which it cannot articulate,—but it divines [that is, learns it by divination, intuits it: *manteuetai*] what it desires, and it riddles about it [*ainittetai*, a verb related to the English "enigma"]. (192c2–d2)

THE DESIRE AND PURSUIT OF THE WHOLE

Next, Aristophanes describes a thought experiment in which a god, Hephaestus the blacksmith, asks a pair of such lovers whether they would like to be physically fused together and made inseparable.

We know that, hearing this, not one person would entirely refuse [the offer], nor would anyone evidently want anything else, but each would absolutely consider himself to have heard the very thing he had yearned for all along: to merge with his lover and be united, from two into one. And the reason is this: that our archaic [that is, original] nature was such [that is, double—like the circle-people, or like the present hypothetical couple fused by Hephaestus], and we were whole. And so *the desire and pursuit of the whole* is called Eros. (192e5–193a1)

Even sex does not bring enough unity, and if Hephaestus were to appear to lovers and offer to forge them into a total union—effectively reversing the punitive surgery of Zeus—they would unanimously accept. Still, we remain under the threat of further divine punishment if we indulge in further hubris: Zeus may just bisect us again, until each of us has to hop around on one leg. But the justice of the gods is not all brutal, since when Zeus visited his surgery upon us, he also brought Eros to help us. Sex is a memorial of the circle-people's hubris against the gods, but it is also the mark of the gods' stewardship over humanity. Zeus split us apart to punish us, but he and Apollo made us sexual in order to preserve us.

The circle-people were fast and strong, and we are to picture them as satisfied: after all, they had as yet no erotic longing for a sundered "other half," and it is this longing that keeps *us* in check. But if they were satisfied, why were they hubristic? If they had all they needed and were not driven by desire and longing, why did they challenge the gods? Sex is a yearning to return to the original wholeness of the circle-people, but if they too were creatures of longing and desire (a cosmic and not a sexual yearning, but a yearning all the same), then even Hephaestus's offer to fuse the lovers permanently would not suffice. This is the way Plato leaves us in need of Diotima's teaching. The hubris of the circle-people gives the lie to Aristophanes' final point: "If we conduct ourselves with due reverence towards the gods, then Eros will restore us to our original nature, healed and blessed with perfect happiness." Diotima will teach that the only happiness that deserves predicates like "perfect" or "final" or "complete" is the one that takes us beyond the body altogether and into contact with the abstract principle of beauty whose reality is greater than that of any one beautiful thing or person. For Aristophanes, a sexual union with one's original soul mate is the perfect happiness, but for Diotima, the value of such a union lies only in its implicit promptings onward toward the beautiful-in-itself, what Plato would go on (in later dialogues) to call the Form of the Beautiful.

Plato never really solved the problem of the relationship between the gods and the Forms, and when Socrates goes to his death in the *Phaedo* he seems to hope to join them both. As moderns, we consider that when Nietzsche (following Schopenhauer) rejected Plato's Forms as mere pipe dreams, he also reconceived the human will as a thing of endlessly unsatisfied striving. From the Nietzschean perspective, the circle-people *had* to challenge the gods, because that hubris was simply the beckoning frontier of their desire. Aristophanes advises us that piety might restore us to wholeness, but—as though that wholeness were not really achievable, and so not our real motive—he also hints that we are only pious for fear of further divine punishment rather than hope of divine aid in becoming whole again.

THE VALIDITY OF DIOTIMA'S DOCTRINE: A LOOK AHEAD

Diotima overcomes Aristophanes' emphasis on finding one's soul mate, since she would have us transcend even the sweetest of our local attachments. But to give them up is to stake everything on an abstraction (the Beautiful itself) that we cannot know until we reach it. What if it is not there? Must we spend our lives "learning to die," as Socrates said every philosopher must, only to find that death *does not* consummate such a life but merely ends it (in which case, we would do no "finding" at all)? Perhaps the local attachments Diotima asks us to give up are our best hope for the only happiness there is. That is the modern worry about Platonism altogether, and it is the theme of Nussbaum's monumental work on ethics, *The Fragility of Goodness*. Of course, if there *are* Forms—or even if there are not, so long as the universe is constituted such that earthly experiences conduce toward a more abstract existence like that of the Forms, for example, a mystical union with the divine—then Diotima's advice is not only good but great, and we can read our interpersonal loves as mere models of a greater, cosmic love beyond them.

Of course, that description makes the validity of Diotima's account depend on the truth or falsehood of its claims about the cosmos: *if* there is an ultimate, supraterrestrial object of our eros (call this object the Form of the Beautiful), such that our contemplation of it might result in the effects Diotima describes (i.e., a climactic vision of transfiguring epistemological power, along with a better fate after death than mere oblivion), *then* her account really is the way eros works. But many of us might continue to feel—even if some special insight were to confirm Diotima's cosmic claims—that human love has little to do with "the Beautiful" and that when, say, Alcestis died for her beloved, she was not motivated by a desire to learn ultimate truths (through a vision of the Beautiful) but merely to benefit the frail human being to whose welfare she felt committed, namely, her lover. Part of Nussbaum's point seems to be this shift in emphasis, during Socrates' speech, from feeling to knowing. In Diotima's discourse, Plato is interested in love insofar as eros drives and informs philosophy. In Alcibiades' speech, Plato is once again interested in eros as a human feeling, and his speech more than any other illuminates the seriousness of the difference between these two conceptions of love.

Now that we have seen something of where we are headed, let us return to the narrative line of *Symposium*. Aristophanes finishes his speech with the remark that only two speakers are left. Eryximachus responds with some flattery to the effect that Socrates and Agathon are prodigious savants in erotics, otherwise Eryximachus would be worried for them lest they come up short—given the number and the variety of the speeches made thus far. This is worth noting as a very early instance of what has since become profoundly familiar—the feeling that literary work is a competition for scarce resources that might run out, and the later the writer, the more difficult his or her position. Keats discussed this feeling in his letters about John Milton, for instance, and Harold Bloom made it the central principle of literary history in his famous study, *The Anxiety of Influence*.[1] Students of literature might therefore find this "Bloomian" moment, in an early text like *Symposium,* somewhat thrilling.

SOCRATES AND AGATHON CONVERSE

Before Agathon's speech gets under way, there is banter between Socrates and the host. Agathon, remember, has just won a public victory (his first and only one) with his first play. The symposium is a drinking party at his house in celebration of that artistic success. Socrates teases Agathon, saying that it should be no trouble to perform in front of a group so much smaller than that huge public crowd Agathon conquered the other day. Agathon replies that, as everyone knows (and performers can still be found admitting this), it is much harder to perform in front of a small group of "the wise" than in front of a large group of everybody else. But Socrates catches up Agathon by probing: What is it that Agathon would feel perfectly all right about doing before the multitude, but that he would be ashamed to do before the present company? This question does not get answered, but the point seems to be that (a) nobody should be content to do anything *unethical* just because he has the right audience for it; but (b) if you do anything *aesthetically* bad—make a bad artistic choice—to suit an audience, that choice must entail an ethical mistake too. We do not get to hear Socrates specify whether this ethical mistake is unfair to the artistic work or to the audience (and one would like to know what he would have said about the question), but we do get the feeling that Socrates' line of reasoning was running in this direction. Socrates' word for badness here is *aischron,* whose primary meaning is "shameful"; that is why he can equivocate so effectively between the ethical and the aesthetic.

8

The Speech of Agathon:
Eros as Young, Beautiful Poet

Agathon was influenced by the fashionable rhetorician Gorgias of
Leontini. His style is therefore ornate and given to punning and plays
on words that do not tend to translate well. The Athenians were
enraptured by Gorgias's style for decades, but modern readers often
find it vexingly superficial.[1] Some critics go so far as to compare
Agathon to the European aesthetes of the 1890s on these grounds.

Agathon takes an allegorical approach to the praise of Eros, and
this involves him in a number of fallacies. Disagreeing with Phaedrus's
claim that Eros is the oldest of the gods, Agathon argues that Eros
"fleeing, flees old age" and must therefore be the youngest of the
gods—"and is always young." If this means that old people do not
burn with erotic desire, Pausanias would seem to be a counter-
example; and if it means that erotic *success* eludes (flees) such old
men, fine—but that does not make Eros young, does it? And if Eros is
"forever (*aiei*) young," then the lateness or earliness of his birth does
not matter much (so Phaedrus is not really wrong about that issue).
Agathon then declares that Eros is sensitive and soft; the evidence for
this claim is that Eros chooses men's characters and souls for his

dwelling place—though when he finds a stubborn, hard ethos, he departs. Note that Agathon may be involved in a tautology here, calling "soft" whichever natures Eros does occupy, and "hard" those natures he shuns.

Having discussed Love's beauty (he settles among those flowers, or among those men, whose bloom is not yet gone), Agathon turns to Love's goodness.

> And if Eros suffers anything, he doesn't suffer from Force (for force doesn't touch Eros), nor does he compel by compulsion: for everyone willingly serves Eros in everything, and whatever is done willingly and by one who consents willingly, 'the laws, [which are] the king of the city,' declare to be just.[2]

Because of the way allegory works, Agathon can make the leap from talking about love (the emotion) to talking about Eros (the god) amid these otherwise logical moves. To remind us of just how false Agathon's conclusion is, we can look ahead to a figure like Virgil's Dido, who at first burns with love's ardor, and later, having been jilted, burns on the pyre of her own suicide. Phaedra, from Euripides' *Hippolytus,* is a more contemporary example of such a person, undone by Love and miserable in its grip. How peculiar, then, that this almost silly optimism should be articulated by a tragic poet—moreover, by a victorious tragic poet, crowned with the bay leaves by the same audience that judged Euripides. Can Agathon have *forgotten* what he knew the other day?

> As for manliness, 'not even Ares can withstand' Eros.[3] For Ares does not hold Eros, but Eros holds Ares—the eros of Aphrodite, as the tale says. Now the one who holds is more powerful than the one who is held; and if the one held is otherwise the most manly among all the mighty, then the holder is the most manly of all. (196c9–d4)

The word I have translated as "manliness" is *andreia*, from a form of the word for man, *andros*. It is usually translated as courage, but that might obscure Agathon's pleasantry in declaring that the god of war is vanquished by the god of love. In the story (from *Odyssey* book 8) to which Agathon refers, Ares and Aphrodite are cheating on Aphrodite's husband, Hephaestus, who snares them both in a net as they make love in bed. That is why Agathon says Eros "holds" Ares; because Ares was emotionally held in love with Aphrodite and because this love got him captured and held in Hephaestus's net. But it is not Eros or Aphrodite who captures them, it is Hephaestus—a god far less reducible to a single function (far less easily allegorized) than Ares (War), or Aphrodite/Eros (Love). In the last sentence of the paragraph above, Agathon completely suppresses the fact that there is more than one way to victory; he suppresses the dichotomy between Achillean *biê* (force) and Odyssean *mêtis* (cleverness) upon which the whole of Homeric poetry is organized. If Eros were the bravest, Paris and Menelaus would be better fighters than their brothers Hector and Agamemnon.

Agathon's argument about Eros's manliness is of a kind known later in Latin as *a fortiori* (from strength): some merely reasonable thing is shown to be true (Ares is usually the most manly), followed by a comparison (Eros turned out to be even more manly than Ares), on the strength of which a new idea is to be inferred (Eros must be the most manly of all).[4] He uses another a fortiori argument to establish Love's wisdom: if Love is responsible for the creation of poets, he himself must be the greatest poet of all, "for the things which one neither has nor knows, one can neither give nor teach to somebody else." This seems reasonable enough, but we should note that at various points Plato denies this idea. Diotima shows us that we get from our lovers a knowledge of the beautiful that does not rest with the lovers or the love but ultimately exists separate from them, in the Beautiful itself. Moreover, in the *Meno*, Plato gives a model of instruction in which a teacher leads a student to the discovery of the student's own forgotten wisdom, not the teacher's.[5] Although the *Meno*'s doctrine of learning-as-recollection is not in play here in *Symposium*, it is important to note that Agathon's a fortiori argument about Eros's wisdom has as its warrant ("you can't teach what you don't know") a proposition that Plato seems to have denied elsewhere.

Agathon applies a similar argument (about Eros as the poet who makes others into poets) to the gods as well: If Apollo invented archery and medicine and music by following his desires and being led by love, then Eros is the real author of these achievements—and not just these achievements of Apollo but also those of the other divinities. In fact, the cruel and amoral Olympian behavior described in Hesiod's *Theogony* (acts like castration and incest, which scandalized Xenophanes and continued to provide matter for anti-Olympian polemics until Augustine's time) happened under the rule of *Anagnkê* (Necessity); once Eros began to rule, such things ceased. It should be clear that this account constitutes a dangerously anti-Olympian outlook, one vulnerable to just the sort of divine retaliation (*nemesis*) that afflicts characters in tragedy, Agathon's own medium. Agathon's beautifully expressed, but chillingly glib, critique of traditional piety adds to our sense of *Symposium* as a work of nostalgic but enlightened hindsight: Between the dramatic date and the writing, history had visited upon Athens, and upon these particular symposiasts, the crushing reversals that redress hubris in the tragedies.

THE RESPONSE TO AGATHON

The company applauded Agathon's speech, we are told, because in it he did credit "to himself and to the god." But the Greek is ambiguous here and can also be saying that Agathon praised himself and Eros. This suggests what we may have been feeling all along: In making Eros out to be a young, beautiful poet, the victorious host is assimilating himself to the god (he does, at 196e, call him *ho Eros agathos,* "Eros the Good," with a pun on his own name).

Socrates claims to have been intimidated by the eloquence of Agathon's finish, and here he makes the punning quotation ("I was afraid ... Gorgias ... Gorgon") from *Odyssey* book 10 that I mentioned in chapter 4. But now Socrates is relieved of his anxiety, because he realizes that the sort of eulogy for which the symposiasts are responsible is not the sort he thought: rather than truth telling, they want a pretty speech. Socrates declares himself incapable of providing that but willing to give a truthful speech instead, in his own way. These claims, which prepare us for Socrates' idiosyncratic mode of expression, echo the very similar claims made at the beginning of the *Apology*.

SOCRATES AND AGATHON CONVERSE AGAIN

Socrates has a second dialogue with Agathon, the point of which is that, by a logical necessity, we can only desire what we do not in fact have. If we seem to do so, we are really only desiring to *continue* having what we have already. But if this is true, Socrates explains, then Eros, who (according to Agathon) loves beauty, cannot be beautiful yet; and because of the close relationship between the beautiful and the good, Eros cannot be good yet either.

9

The Speech of Socrates: Diotima, the Itinerant Priestess, Explains Eros

We are now in the region of *Symposium* with perhaps the greatest claim on our philosophical and literary attention. The speeches of Socrates and Alcibiades are the most significant in the dialogue, and this is ironic because neither Diotima (the main speaker in Socrates' speech) nor Alcibiades was present when the symposium got started and the charge was given to speak a speech in praise of Eros.

Socrates explains that Diotima was responsible for delaying the plague at Athens by 10 years. This medical-religious feat is profoundly pragmatic, rather like Eryximachus's treatment of Aristophanes' hiccups. Note that whereas Eryximachus's bit of practice was really based on waiting for the affliction (hiccups) to go away, Diotima's amounted to postponing it (plague), so that the two are ironic opposites. Just as the doctor's skill was supported by a theory (the pre-Socratic physics he articulates), Diotima's ability to postpone the plague is to be imagined as the natural result of the wisdom she articulates in Socrates' speech, which is primarily a long quotation from her.

The Speech of Socrates

We do indeed get a dialectic from Socrates, as in the other Platonic dialogues, but this time Socrates is the student, and the teacher is Diotima (whose name means "Zeus's honor"). It takes as its point of departure the same exchange Socrates has just had with Agathon.[1] When the philosopher took the position that Eros was beautiful, Diotima explained that Eros was not, as Socrates has just done with Agathon. "But surely Eros is not on that account shameful and bad?" asks Socrates. Diotima's response begins with a warning, in a Greek idiom ("won't you speak well?!") that means "watch what you say!" This anxiety over the possibility of blasphemous speech sets a more pious tone than what we found in the preceding speeches and puts us in mind of the dangers of verbal hubris.

Eros is not shameful or ugly merely because he is not yet beautiful. Desiring the beautiful, he is *in between* the beautiful and the ugly. There is a middle ground between the two, just as there is a middle ground between knowledge and ignorance. The latter middle ground is what we call "true belief," namely, when a person is aware of what is true but not yet certain that his opinion is indeed the right one. As the text puts it, such a person is not yet "capable of giving an account" of what he nevertheless rightly believes.

Since Eros does not yet possess beauty and goodness, he must not quite be a god either. With this step Diotima establishes that there is an intermediate category between mortals and gods, namely the *daimon*. This argues, albeit on different grounds, the point made variously by Eryximachus, Aristophanes, and Agathon: that Eros regulates the relations between men and gods. Diotima tells us that "between men and gods, Eros interprets and carries messages, prayers, and sacrifices; occupying the space between men and gods, he binds all into a whole" (202e). This "occupying the space" is meant literally, since the gods dwell above and the men beneath (and as Agathon says, Eros walks on our heads). But its main sense is taxonomic (Eros is in a category between mortal and immortal). We should remember Aristophanes when Diotima tells us that Eros binds the world into a whole: whereas Zeus began Eros by dividing the circle-people in half, here Eros (like the other *daimones*) unites not only the sundered human beings but the whole of humanity and divinity and, thereby, the whole cosmos.

FIRST MYTH: EROS'S ORIGIN

Asked about Eros's parentage, Diotima tells a story (that is, she speaks a myth, as Aristophanes did but Agathon did not). "When Aphrodite was born, they were celebrating, the gods and others, and *Mêtis* [Cunning], whose child was *Poros* [Plenty or Means]" (203b). "Poros" means a way forward, and so metaphorically either "contrivance" or "plenty of money." It is what one lacks when one is stuck in *aporia,* the state of being "at a loss." Note that *Mêtis* is what Odysseus has in abundance ("*polymêtis* Odysseus"), so that while Diotima is as allegorical as Agathon here, her allegory centers on what Agathon had suppressed (i.e., the opposition between *mêtis* [cunning] and *biê* [force]). It also picks up overtones of the relationship between Socrates and Odysseus suggested earlier.

As might be expected at a feast, Poverty, being in *aporia* as usual, came in to beg, and when she found Poros sleeping in the garden and drunk with nectar, she lay down with him and conceived Eros. Eros became the companion of Aphrodite because he was engendered on her birthday, and because by nature Eros is a lover of beauty, and Aphrodite is beautiful. Since he is the child of Poverty and Plenty, he is always poor, and, quite far from the opinion that he is delicate and lovely, held by the many (and here the Socratic irony is at Agathon's expense, since he holds this opinion, too, and we have already heard Agathon's contempt for "the many"), Eros is in fact hard and in a squalid condition, homeless and (like Socrates and his fans) shoeless. He is not totally poor but close to it, and he can never get out of that economic middle ground. As the list of Eros's attributes continues, it makes him sound more and more like Socrates. Just as Eros is between mortal and immortal, he is also between knowledge and ignorance, and in this state he loves knowledge, knowing that so far his wisdom consists only in the awareness that he needs more. That was, of course, Socrates' claim about himself in the *Apology*. We are reminded that the word *philosophy* literally means "love of wisdom."

EROS'S OBJECT: THE PERPETUAL POSSESSION OF THE GOOD

"Let me try to teach you the next point," says Diotima (204d). "Eros' generation and nature are such as we've said, but as you point out, there is also his love of beauty. And what would we say if somebody should ask us, 'Why does Eros love what's beautiful, O Socrates and Diotima?' or more clearly, 'He loves beautiful things: *why* does he love them?'" "To possess them," Socrates answers.[2]

"But this answer [*apokrisis*] longs for the following question [*erotêsis*]: what is it that comes to someone to whom beautiful things come?" Here there is more than a hint of the erotic nature of philosophy, since *apokrisis* means both "an answer" and "a separating," like the one that began Eros in Aristophanes' speech (by separating the halves of the circle-people), and the word for "question," *erotêsis*, contains a pun on Eros. The question "yearns for" the answer.

Socrates finds this form of the question too difficult, so Diotima rephrases it in terms of goodness instead of beauty. "Someone who loves good things—for what does he love them?" And the same answer is given: "To possess them." "And what does a person gain if he gains the good things?" "That question," says Socrates, "I'm more readily able to answer: he'll be happy." "For the happy are happy in the possession of the good things," Diotima responds, "so that there's no need to go on to ask *why he desires to be happy*, who so desires. Instead, your answer seems quite final" (205a).

The word for "final" here is *telos*, "an endpoint, a purpose." Now, late in his writing life, Nietzsche denied that there was such a thing as closure in human desiring and declared instead that not only human nature but all nature is characterized by an inherently endless striving. The hubris of the circle-people, like the fall of Satan in Milton's *Paradise Lost*, supports Nietzsche's claim, since those stories show creatures grasping for more than the apparently complete portions they already possess. While Diotima's point (that happiness is an end in itself) seems self-evident, it also seems to imply an account of human desire as finite (which is not, from our perspective, self-evident). But those of us who do not agree with her may later change our minds, when Diotima furnishes our desire with an object so self-sufficient and inexhaustible that we can well image that a person who found it would seek no further.

To resume, Diotima's next point is that *everybody* desires to possess the good things forever, and therefore everybody is, in this sense, a lover. Just as we only use the word *poem* to refer to a verbal artifact made in verse, while the fuller sense of the word *poem* is simply "artifact," so we commonly use the word *love* to refer to a particular kind of love, denoting the other kinds by other names. "And a certain argument is sometimes made," continues Diotima, almost as though she had heard the speech of Aristophanes,

> that lovers search for the sundered half of a complete whole. But my argument says that love is neither of a half, nor of a whole, unless of course, my friend, that half or whole should happen to be the Good—since men would willingly cut off their own hands and feet, if they thought those appendages were bad. For they do not cling to their own things, unless they call their own things good, and those of others, bad. What men love is nothing but the Good. Or doesn't it seem so to you? (205d10–206a1)

Cutting off one's own corrupt hands and feet compromises one's wholeness; but if those appendages are "bad" enough, amputation becomes a serious option (as in Jesus' remark, "if thy right eye offend thee, pluck it out," where the badness is not medical gangrene but moral laxity). Having established that love is not of wholeness per se but of the Good, Diotima goes on to specify that it is no use possessing the Good only to lose it later; what we all really want is *the perpetual possession of the Good* (206a11). When we translate literally "Eros is of the Good," we mean that Eros has the Good as its object, or in other words, that in loving, one is really loving the Good.

The Speech of Socrates

EROS'S PURPOSE: PROCREATION IN THE BEAUTIFUL

At this point the prophetess makes a new step in her argument: Love turns out to have a deeper purpose even than the perpetual possession of the Good, namely, procreation in the Beautiful. The former is a mere holding; the latter is creative.

"Since this Love is always this [that is, is always the pursuit of the perpetual possession of the Good]," she said, "in what manner, and in what activity, ought the zeal and effort of those pursuing it be called Love? What's the point of that effort? Can you tell me?"[3]

"I certainly can't tell you. If I could," I answered, "I wouldn't be so amazed at your wisdom, Diotima; as it is, I come to you in order to learn from you these very things."[4]

"Then I'll tell you. It is procreation in the beautiful, both of the body and of the soul."

"I need divination for whatever it is you're saying; right now I'm not learning it."

"Then I'll say it more clearly," she said. "All human beings procreate in the body and in the soul, and when they come to a certain time of life—the very nature of us desires to give birth. And it can't give birth in the ugly, but only in the beautiful. Yes, and the sexual union of the woman and the man is itself a birth. And it [sex] is a divine affair—for this is the immortality of animals [*zôo*, "things that live"], though they're mortal: procreation and birth. But it's impossible to conceive in the presence of what's unsuitable. And the ugly is entirely unsuitable to the divine, whereas the beautiful is suitable. And so *Moira* ["portion, fate," sometimes invoked as a childbirth goddess], and *Eileithuia* [the specific goddess of childbirth], and Beauty herself, are present at genesis. That is why, when what is pregnant comes near to beauty, whatever is pregnant becomes gracious, and pours itself forth, delighted, and gives birth and procreates. Whereas amid what is ugly, it broods[5] and is distressed, and shrinks back, and turns away and is repulsed, and doesn't give birth, so the pregnancy is very difficult to bear.[6] This is why, in the presence of beauty, a great passionate excitement befalls a person who's already swelling with pregnancy—because beauty delivers the person from the prodigious pains of labor.[7] And so Eros is not of the beautiful, as you think it is."

"Of what, then?"

"Of procreation and birth in the beautiful."

"Very well."

"Oh, most definitely. And why is it of procreation? Because procreation is the [only form of] immortality and endless life available to mortals." (206b1–e8)

EROS IS OF IMMORTALITY

Next, at 207a, Diotima reintroduces "permanent possession of the good" in order to combine it with "procreation in the beautiful," merging the two formulations of Love's goal into a single expression:

> Given the things we've agreed upon, one necessarily desires immortality with the Good, since Eros is of the good one would *permanently* possess. Indeed, it's necessary from this line of reasoning that *Eros is of immortality.* (206e8–207a4)

IMMORTALITY BY REPLACEMENT: THE CONTINUITY OF THE GENERATIONS

Diotima cites examples from the animal world, illustrating the power of the urge to reproduce and to see that one's offspring thrive. Lovesickness continues long after reproduction; it emboldens the weakest animals to fight against even the strongest, in order to protect their young (and this is reminiscent of Phaedrus's army of lovers). Animals and people go to these lengths because the begetting of children is a kind of immortality, by which the current generation replaces itself with its offspring. Now, in case we feel that this immortality is not enough, because the individual does not survive, Diotima incisively examines our common notion of individual existence and finds that it, too, is an affair of continual replacement: like the human population, an individual body is always in flux, and the skin, hair, blood, bones, and flesh, and indeed the whole body, are always dying and being replaced. Remarkably (*atopôteron*, "more strange yet than this" [207e5]), she explains, this is true of the individual *mind* as well: thoughts, memories, and skills are always being lost and regained through practice and experience (we referred to this in a section of chapter 3 called "The Wool Analogy"). A god is not in flux this way, but mortals must be, since we are always perishing.

PHILOTIMIA (THE LOVE OF HONOR) IS REALLY THIS SAME LOVE OF IMMORTALITY

Diotima quotes a hexameter line of poetry whose source we have lost: "to establish for all time their immortal fame." That is what people try to do who are obsessed with prestige—people like Alcestis and Achilles (these were the very persons adduced by Phaedrus in his speech, so we may well wonder whether Socrates is really improvising this whole story about Diotima or at least modifying it to suit the occasion). Such people will make tremendous sacrifices for honor, spending their money, enduring hardships, and even risking their lives to gain it (and this foreshadows the entrance of Alcibiades, whose career was summarized in chapter 1); they are in love with immortality (208e).

DIVERSE KINDS OF PREGNANCY

Those men who are primarily pregnant in the body are primarily attracted to women, and they hope to gain happiness and immortality through the begetting of children. But others are more pregnant in the soul than in the body, and accordingly, they bring forth mental offspring. Of these mentally fertile men Diotima gives three examples: the poets and craftsmen, the statesmen, and the lovers. The lovers she means are those who foster one another's education, discussing virtue and the practices that are necessary for a man to be good. Since virtue, and this shared discourse about it, are already a part of immortality, the relationships that engender virtue and virtuous discourse are more intense and enduring than those that engender merely human children. In support of this, Diotima points to our common enthusiasm for the achievements of the famous poets and statesmen (Homer and Hesiod; Lycurgus and Solon) whose offspring will clearly endure forever: such people "perform many beautiful deeds, having begotten all sorts of excellence." This turn of phrase, and indeed the whole argument, involves an equivocation between the beautiful and the good. Earlier (209a), she called statecraft "by far the greatest and the most beautiful" among the various creativities of those pregnant in soul, but in her short list of examples (209c) we may feel that the poets fare no worse than the statesmen. Both achieve a greater share of immortality than biological fatherhood or motherhood can confer.

The good is self-sufficient: to possess it forever constitutes the happiness that Socrates and Diotima take to be an end in itself. But no mortal can possess the good forever, at least not by any normal means, and so we procreate instead; procreation is as close as mortals can approach to immortality. But it turns out that a certain kind of procreation—namely, procreation *from* the soul and *in* the beautiful—can lead us beyond the normal means to which we had been limited. Whereas the good (whose perpetual possession requires an immortality we do not have) is final but ultimately unavailable, the beautiful is available and conducive: it leads us onward, and Eros is the lover's intrepid following where beauty leads.

THE GREATER MYSTERIES

Using the language of initiation into the Mystery cult of Eleusis, Diotima makes a break in her argument at 210a: Socrates can probably be initiated into those mysteries of erotica that Diotima has discussed so far, but she doubts that he could handle the next part. To do so would be "to see those ultimate sights, for which the preceding things were [merely the required prelude]." The term for those sights is *ta epoptika* (the things looked-upon), and somebody who sees them is an initiate of the high religious rank called *epoptês*, often translated

"Watcher." We do not know just what the real Watchers were seeing in the Mystery cult centered in the shrine at Eleusis, largely because the Mystery religions of ancient Greece were so secretive (and have long since disappeared). But what follows is Plato's metaphorical use of the ritual forms of piety for his own philosophical purposes. To what degree this represents Plato's interpretation of historically real Mystery religion nobody can say, though Michael Morgan's *Platonic Piety* is a stimulating exploration of that issue.[8] Plato certainly seems to be claiming, in the climax of *Symposium* we are about to discuss, that philosophical growth is like religious initiation and that both eventuate in a transcendence of our mortal, human condition. As we try to come to grips with the doctrinal nuances of her speech, we should bear in mind that Diotima the priestess is a problem solver, who used her wisdom effectively to postpone the arrival of plague in Athens by 10 years. Religious knowledge of that kind is as pragmatic as it is profound, and she speaks to Socrates about Eros as though there were no distinction (at least, none from the wise person's perspective) between piety and philosophy: the ladder of ascent is simply the way it works.

THE LADDER OF ASCENT

The final revelation is "that, for the sake of which, there exists what has preceded it"; in other words, everything we have heard so far (i.e., everything we have heard up to this point from Diotima—but since Socrates is narrating, he is also ironically referring to the preceding speeches of the present company) is just a prelude to it. The climax of *Symposium* is Diotima's account of the following ordered series of stages in erotic wisdom; and the climax of that account is the final stage of the series:

1. "A lover should begin, when young, desiring the beauty of the body; and, if his guide guides him aright, he should love one particular body, and beget beautiful discourse on it;" (210a)

2. "but then, realizing that the beauty of that body is akin to other bodily beauties, he would be foolish not to regard the beauties of all beautiful bodies as one and the same;" (210b)

3. "and since he realizes that, he must become a lover of all such beautiful bodies; and now he contemns his zealous love for one bodily beauty, and regards it as trivial;"

4. "thereafter he regards the beauty of souls as more honorable than that of bodies;"

5. "so that the presence of someone of appropriate soul, even if he's lacking in youthful bloom, suffices for the lover to love him and care for him, and beget the sort of edifying speeches which cause young people to improve," (210c)

6. "in order that he may be compelled to see the beauty in laws and practices, and to see that the beauties among these beautiful laws and practices are all the same,"

7. "in order that he come to consider bodily beauty a trivial thing,"

8. "and after the beauty of practices, the lover must lead the beloved to the sciences, in order that he may perceive the beauty of them," (210c7)

9. "and, seeing the manifold of beauty instead of slavishly being content with the single beauty of a handsome boy, or man, or of some single practice, like a petty and inarticulate boor—instead of this, turning to the great sea of beauty and regarding there many beautiful and magnificent discourses, he begets great thoughts in unfettered love of wisdom" (210d)

10. "until, emboldened and fortified at this point, he understands a kind of knowledge which is singular, the beauty of which is as follows...."

A NOTE ON THE GRAMMAR OF POINT SIX

So far, this list translates (and is) one enormous sentence. The conjunction that begins point 6 is *hina,* and it usually introduces a purpose clause and means "in order that." Since we know we are hearing about the lover's process of ascent, we expect a result clause introduced by *hôste* (with the result that): the lover begets edifying speeches *with the result that* the lover is compelled to go the next step up the ladder by contemplating the beauty of laws and practices. But Plato gives us a purpose clause: "the lover begets edifying speeches *in order that* he be compelled," etc. But how can the lover purposively plan to compel himself? The right construction might be this: the lover begets edifying speeches in order that the *beloved* (who is being edified by the lover's speeches) be compelled to contemplate the beauty of laws and practices. This way, the lover gets to the next stage precisely by teaching the beloved—either because the lover has discovered the beauty of laws and practices in the course of making his speeches, and goes on to speak about those newly discovered beauties, or because the lover's begetting-in-beauty is brought forward to the critical point only when and if he compels the beloved to contemplate the beauty of laws and practices.

LEARNING BY TEACHING

Similarly, point 7 was already achieved—for the lover—in point 4. Might it be the beloved who, once again, is being enlightened in point 7? Editors and commentators remark upon the grammar of point 8, rightly insisting that the subject of the verb "lead" (the one doing the leading) cannot be the beloved. Some (e.g., Dover [1980], Rose) read the subject as the "guide" who began the process in point 1 and then disappeared. The advantage of that reading is that it gives us only one student, the lover, whose career we follow from beginning to fulfillment. But part of Plato's point in writing this ambiguity—for he can be as unambiguous as he likes—seems to be that the teacher is simultaneously a student, and he graduates only by bringing a younger person along with or behind him. As translated above, this list has three characters: (a) the older guide who appears only in point 1 and sets the young lover going; (b) the young lover who himself becomes an older guide in the course of the journey; and (c) the new, young beloved whom the lover (b) educates.

Note that Socrates' contempt, in point 9, for those who esteem "only one practice" accords well with his notorious antagonism against "experts" of all kinds. As he explains in the *Apology*, Socrates routinely cross-examined various professionals, those who professed expertise in a single discipline like horse training or generalship, or rhapsody or rhetoric, and exposed their hidden ignorance. To be an expert in a single practice is usually to ignore its foundations, those underlying parts of the practice that blend into deeper, philosophical questions that transcend expertise.

THE FINAL REVELATION

"And now pay attention as much as you can," Diotima continues,

> For when he has been educated in the matters of Eros to this extent, having seen various beauties accurately and one after another, coming now to the fulfillment [*telos*] of erotics he suddenly [*exaiphnês*] perceives the astounding nature of The Beautiful, that very thing for the sake of which were all his previous labors. First of all, it is eternal, neither coming-to-be nor passing-away, neither growing up nor perishing, since it isn't beautiful only in one place but ugly in another, nor beautiful at some time but not at some other time, nor beautiful in some circumstance but ugly in some other, nor beautiful to somebody but ugly to someone else. Nor will it appear to him as the beauty of a face, nor of hands, nor of anything else pertaining to the body, nor of a discourse nor of a knowledge, nor as a beauty dependent on any other thing, whether living being, or anything of earth or heaven or elsewhere—but it exists eternally itself unto itself alone; and all other beautiful things partake of it, in such a manner that when they grow or perish, it doesn't increase or diminish but remains unaffected. (210d7–211b5)

The remainder of Diotima's talk is a recapitulation of what we have heard, with the instruction that Socrates should ascend from one kind of beauty to the next "as though using a ladder" (211c3). The frame of reference is still paiderasty, but now Diotima has made clear that the loving admiration of beautiful bodies is only an initial spur and not at all the real goal of the lover's development. This should give erotic hope to Socrates, who was not considered a handsome person, and it also implies (what Aristophanes has already said) that the fundamental nature of eros is by no means limited to paiderasty.

Diotima does seem to insist, however, that the love of the beautiful body is a necessary beginning, a stage we cannot skip. But there is some question as to whether Socrates has skipped it. If Socrates ever arrives at the vision of the Beautiful, she explains, he will become quite impervious to the beauty of handsome boys—by whom he now finds himself dumbstruck with infatuation. In the final speech of *Symposium*, we hear Alcibiades tell a story in which the young, beautiful aristocrat tries to seduce the older (much older than he was with Diotima) and uglier philosopher—without success. Has Socrates ignored Diotima's advice, and remained a nonlover? Or has he progressed so far, in the long meantime, as to be finished with handsome youths and their distracting charms? Remember that at 177d Socrates said, "I claim to know nothing but the things of love [*ta erotika*]."

> "And that is where, if anywhere, dear Socrates," said the woman from Mantinea, "human life is to be lived: in the contemplation of the Beautiful." (211d1)

> "And if indeed it should happen to someone—to see pure Beauty itself, unmixed, unalloyed, neither filled-in with flesh nor with human nature, nor with colors, and free of all the other extraneous features of mortality—what would we expect if someone were able to see Beauty itself, divine and unitary? Do you suppose that a human being who gazes thereon (with that by which one *must* gaze thereon[9]), and dwells therein, leads a trivial life? Or don't you rather feel, that it is only there—by his seeing (with that by which it can be seen) the sight of Beauty—that it will befall him to beget, not images of virtue, since he does not touch upon mere images, but the truth, since he grasps what is true? And that by begetting and nourishing true virtue, and through love of the gods, it might accrue to him, too—if to any among mankind—to become immortal?"

> Those are indeed the things Diotima said, Phaedrus and you others, and I'm convinced. And being so convinced, I also try to convince others that for the achievement[10] of this goal, one could not easily find a better ally for human nature than Eros. Therefore I hold it necessary that all men honor Eros, and I myself honor and practice erotics zealously[11] and I exhort others to do so, and now and always I praise the power and manly courage of Eros as much as I am able. And so, Phaedrus, consider *that* to be

my speech spoken in praise of Eros, if you will; but if you're pleased to call it something else, call it what you please. (211d8–212c3)

Eros is a philosopher not unlike Socrates, so it should not surprise us that the goal of love is not intimacy with another human being per se but intimacy with the Beautiful and a consequent intimacy with the gods that might eventuate in immortality. This paradigm is profoundly familiar to modern readers, but not as an account of human love. *Symposium*'s religious rhetoric of ascent has been absorbed and transformed by Christianity (via Plotinus), Judaism (in the Neoplatonism of the Kabalah), and Islam (especially in the works of Ibn Arabi, which probably influenced Dante's *Paradiso*).[12] But as an account of the love between human sexual partners, Diotima's speech remains strange and counterintuitive; accordingly, modern readers, who often bring to *Symposium* a serious and multivalent wariness about Platonic appeals to "the Absolute," are drawn instead to the speeches of Aristophanes and Alcibiades. Depending on the nature and degree of our dissent from Platonism, we may feel that they constitute a truer vision of the human situation. From the point of view of the Platonic tradition, however, Diotima's speech is the peak that rises above the other speeches philosophically and rhetorically; furthermore, the discourse of Diotima has a certain narrative eroticism that lends intuitive support to its description of eros. Each of the symposiasts discusses sexuality, to be sure; but Diotima's speech rises and falls in narrative intensity in a way that implicitly parallels the sexuality it describes.[13]

10

The Speech of Alcibiades:
Socrates the Inscrutable

DIONYSUS SHALL BE OUR ARBITRATOR

"Socrates finished speaking; there was applause, and Aristophanes, remembering that his own speech had been mentioned, was trying to say something—but then suddenly [*exaiphnês*] they heard a knocking at the outer-door and the sound of revelers, and the voice of a flute-girl." Agathon invites the new guests inside when it becomes clear that their leader is Alcibiades, drunk and crowned with ivy and violets and calling "Where is Agathon? Lead me to Agathon!"

The crown of ivy, and the drunkenness, make Alcibiades a figure for Dionysus, the god of wine and of ecstasy and of the theater. His arrival interrupts Aristophanes, but we remember Eryximachus's remark that Aristophanes "is all about Aphrodite and Dionysus," that is, sex and drink; and since Aristophanes has already discussed sex, it is fitting that the other half of his usual subject matter should come walking in the door just as he opens his mouth.

Alcibiades announces that he intends to crown Agathon with the wreaths from his own head; a few phrases later, he says he intends to crown "the wisest and most beautiful one," still referring to Agathon. He asks whether they will drink with him or no, and Agathon agrees on behalf of the whole symposium, giving Alcibiades a seat between him and Socrates. But Alcibiades does not notice Socrates' presence yet, because he is busy undoing the wreaths, which fall in front of his eyes for a moment. Then, startled, he cries out that Socrates has been waiting in ambush for him, as usual, appearing suddenly [*exaiphnês*] where he least expects him to be. It is worth noting that these are the three occurrences of this word *exaiphnês* in *Symposium*: the sudden appearance of the vision of the Beautiful in Diotima's discourse (210e4), the sudden arrival of Alcibiades and his party just when the circle of speeches would otherwise have been formally complete (212c6), and the sudden appearance of Socrates (who, like the Beautiful, was already there) to Alcibiades on the couch (213c1).

At this point Alcibiades and Socrates exchange some very witty jibes whose level of irony is hard to specify. "See if you can protect me, Agathon," Socrates says, "for my love for this man has become no small matter to me: ever since the time when I first fell in love with him, I can't look at or speak with a single handsome man, or he [Alcibiades] becomes jealous, and envious, and does remarkable things, railing at me, stopping just short of laying his hands on me ..."(213d3). We find this funny at first, since Socrates is at the other extreme from Alcibiades' legendary gorgeousness. In calling the beautiful, popular Alcibiades a jealous lover, Socrates is really making fun of himself—for how could a man with a face like a stingray reduce the great Alcibiades to jealousy? And yet we are about to hear the story of his failure to seduce Socrates. Therefore, whereas Socrates' remark *seems* to be (a) ironically accusing a self-sufficient Alcibiades of jealousy and (b) ironically portraying the ugly Socrates as a hard-to-get catch, we learn later that Alcibiades is indeed in love with Socrates and indeed unable to seduce him. Therefore the jibe is not innocent and jocular but a painful spur, by which Socrates may hope to hurt Alcibiades into the kind of self-sufficiency that Diotima ultimately recommended.

"There can be no truce between you and me," Alcibiades responds, "but I'll revenge myself upon you in the future, for those remarks." After this initial hostility, Alcibiades takes back some of the wreaths with which he had crowned Agathon and uses them to crown Socrates, "since he triumphs over all men with words, not only the-day-before-yesterday, like you [Agathon], but always." So the intention to crown "the wisest and most beautiful head," which Alcibiades announced back at 212e8, is fulfilled here at 213e2 in a way that gives those great predicates not to Agathon (whom Alcibiades had in mind at 212e8) nor to Eros (the subject of the evening's praise speeches) but to Socrates.

Note also that at 175e, Agathon told Socrates that Dionysus would judge between the two of them, as to which one was wiser; here is Alcibiades, drunk with wine and crowned with Dionysian ivy, surrounded by attendants just as the god is attended by his Maenads, and he crowns—Socrates. This confirms Agathon's concession of his own defeat at 201c.

The Archonship of the Symposium: Alcibiades and Eryximachus

After the crownings, Alcibiades' next affair is to dominate the symposium. Part of the conventions of such drinking parties was the appointment (generally at the beginning of the gathering) of an *archon*, or president, who set the proportions of wine to water, made obligatory toasts at his own discretion, and probably took charge of the conversation. Though Eryximachus has taken on most of these functions since the beginning, tonight's symposium has been unusually democratic in that nobody has ordered anyone else to drink. Now Alcibiades pushes against that fragile arrangement: "You all seem to me to be sober—that's not allowed; you've got to drink. So I'll choose someone to rule on your drinking, as to when you've drunk sufficiently: me!" Like his distribution of the honorific crowns, this grasping at the (trivial) archonship of the symposium is a comic (because miniaturized) version of the very real hubris Alcibiades showed in his later public career. He then serves himself an enormous portion of unmixed wine and has the servant do the same for Socrates.[1]

ALCIBIADES PRAISES NOT EROS BUT SOCRATES

The outcome of these brief negotiations is that whereas the others have each praised Eros, Alcibiades is to praise Socrates. He protests that his aim is not to mock the philosopher but to speak the truth about him, and Socrates reluctantly consents to be praised on that condition. Readers of the *Apology* may hear an echo of Socrates' familiar insistence upon speaking the truth (which also occurred at *Symposium* 198d–199b, where Socrates declared he would not make a traditional encomium to Eros but would "speak the truth" instead). This truth turns out to be mostly praise, though Alcibiades is also frustrated and bemused by his former mentor.

ALCIBIADES SPEAKS IN *EIKONÔN* (IMAGES)

I will try, men, to praise Socrates like so: through images. Maybe this fellow will find my remarks comic, but I use these images for the sake of the truth, not of laughter. For I declare that he most closely resembles one of those *Silenoi* [a kind of satyr, with a snub nose and narrow eyes] in the shops of the statue-makers; the sculptors make them holding a flute or a *syrinx* [musical pipes], and when they're opened into two halves, they reveal statues of the gods held inside them. I also say that he resembles the satyr Marsyas.[2] At any rate that's what your face is like, Socrates—you can't deny it. And you're like them in other ways, which you'll hear next: you're hubristic. Aren't you? If you disagree, I'll furnish witnesses. You don't play the flute? But you're more amazing [at it] than that one [Marsyas]. He enchants people with the power that comes from his mouth, and even today, whoever plays his music (I'd say Olympus played Marsyas's music, and was taught by him), whether a fine flute-man or a trivial flute-girl, it alone causes possession, and shows who is in need of the gods and the Mystery-rites—because it [Marsyas's music] is divine. You differ from him only in one respect: that without any instrument you work the same effects with your bare words. (215a4–d1)

Alcibiades compares Socrates to one of those deceptive statues of the Silenus that open up to reveal hidden statues of the gods. He then compares him to Marsyas, the hubristic satyr who challenged Apollo and lost. These two comparisons are very suggestive, for several reasons:

1. As we discussed in chapter 1, Alcibiades will soon be accused of the serious religious crime of desecrating the Herms, small guardian statues of Hermes the god of travel. The word for statue maker in this speech is *hermoglypheios* (maker of Herms).

2. Marsyas was *flayed* by Apollo as punishment for his hubristic competition with divinity. Socrates was put on trial and executed for crimes that are sometimes interpreted as hubristic along these lines: The conservatives were worried that philosophy was becoming a competitor to traditional piety. The flaying of Marsyas is consistent with the opening up of the Silenus statue to disclose the divine statuettes inside; both are images of the revelation of what had been hidden inside an exceptional (i.e., hubristic) individual. A venturesome interpretation might claim that what Socrates invented, over the course of his career, was indeed a new kind of interiority, an inner life enabled by philosophy (and more particularly, by Socratic irony).[3]

3. On the contrary, although Alcibiades' metaphor of the hidden statues is spoken in praise of Socrates, it may suggest that there is something uncanny, nonliving, sterile about Socrates. He seems like one of those statues, which open up to reveal—more statues. At 219a2, Socrates will warn Alcibiades, "But, O blessed one, examine more carefully, lest it escape your notice that I am nothing." The idiomatic meaning of "I am nothing" here is "I have nothing to offer" or "I'm of no account." But the suggestion is that, as Nussbaum has argued, Socrates has made himself so independent of human relationship that he has become something not quite human: like a statue (or a remote god). This accords with his invulnerability to Alcibiades' sexual charms (216c4–219d2), to the cold (219d3–220c1), and to any distraction from his own thoughts (220c2–d5).

Finally Alcibiades' anecdotes begin, and it is here that we get the best of Plato's personal impressions of his old master. It is hard to remember that Plato is the person writing these lines, since Alcibiades the speaker is as fascinating as Socrates the subject:

> Even now I realize that if I were to open my ears to him, I wouldn't be able to hold out; I'd undergo the same things all over again. For he compels me to agree, that I'm busy with Athenian affairs while I neglect my own deficiencies. And so I stop up my ears by force and flee, as if from the Sirens, lest I sit at his feet until I grow old. (216a3–a9)

Note that Alcibiades does not consider the possibility of a terminable education, one that would end when the student had achieved adequate preparation for political life. Instead, the only alternatives seem to be reckless adventurism (Alcibiades' eventual fate, from the Platonic point of view) at one extreme and at the other, the interminable discipleship that a man of action would have deplored in a person like Plato—who put aside politics for philosophy and "sat at Socrates' feet until old age," as Alcibiades feared to do.[4] The Platonic irony here is that had Alcibiades chosen philosophy, he too might have lived to be old. The comparison to the Sirens is particularly apt, because Odysseus fled from them in order to remain a man of action; this is just what Alcibiades is trying to do in avoiding the philosophical burdens of which Socrates reminds him. Like the Muses, the Sirens had a kind of omniscience, and they seduced sailors by singing songs about the sailors' past accomplishments: They address Odysseus in *Odyssey* book 12, "Bring your ship in ... For we know everything endured in wide Troy." Had he not lashed himself to the mast, Odysseus would have remained until death on the Sirens' island, absorbed in songs of his own past deeds. But the young Alcibiades of this anecdote has as yet few deeds to his credit, and a Socratic examination of "myself," however needful it may be, seems to threaten Alcibiades with obscurity: Introspection and dialectic leave no time for the achievement of victories and fame, the only form of personal identity he finds ultimately convincing. So Alcibiades' choice is not between the seduction of Socratic philosophy and some sober freedom of his own; his choice is rather between two kinds of seduction, the philosophical and the popular:

> I'm affected by this man as by no other, in a way which one might think was impossible for me, namely, to be ashamed (at all). But I

do feel shame before him—and him only. For I know I'm incapable of countering his arguments, of claiming that the things he
enjoins upon me aren't necessary—but when I've parted from
him, *I succumb to the honor of the multitude.* (216a8–b5)

How did the courtship between Socrates and Alcibiades begin? It had
something to do with the younger man's love of wisdom: "Believing
that he was zealous for my youthful beauty, I thought myself very fortunate and marveled at my prodigious good luck, expecting that by
gratifying Socrates, I would be able to hear from him whatever it was
that he knew." Alcibiades here at 217a sounds a lot like Agathon at
175c: in each case, a younger, more handsome man is attracted to
Socrates in the belief that wisdom is something easily transferred from
one person to another. But what follows makes clear to him the real
difficulty of becoming wise, how it requires us to give up the apparently urgent desires that would otherwise continue to distract us, and
this is beyond Alcibiades' power. Like Agathon, he is seduced by the
adulation of the masses, whereas Socrates, who is indifferent to such
honors, can only speak effectively to one person at a time.

This fits well with our impression of Socrates at his trial in the
Apology, where his long speech in his own defense failed to win him
acquittal, and in the *Protagoras,* where he insists that because of a
weak memory he cannot trade long speeches with the rhetorician but
must use his accustomed form of question and answer instead. If this
is so, we can expect that Socrates' real nature will become apparent
only in the kind of intimate exchange Alcibiades describes, and that
the public impression of the man will be only a convenient and ironic
mask. This also explains why Plato (through his character Alcibiades)
employs language reminiscent of the Eleusinian Mysteries in discussing this split between an esoteric (secret) Socrates and an exoteric
(public) one: Mystery religion is articulated through precisely this
kind of split (with a god or gods in the center, where Alcibiades'
speech has put Socrates: "none of you knows him"). As we discussed
in the historical essay at the start of this book, Alcibiades was accused
by his political rivals of having violated the boundary between the
exoteric and the esoteric in revealing religious secrets to the uniniti-

ated (and then, in a separate but similar accusation, they claimed it was Alcibiades and his friends [including Eryximachus!] who had mutilated the Herms). Therefore, by putting the rhetoric of the Mysteries into Alcibiades' speech about Socrates, Plato can be understood to be making a profound comparison between religion and philosophy, one he would make again in different terms in later works like the *Republic*.

SOCRATES IS MYSTERIOUS

Alcibiades was sexually rejected by Socrates, and it ended their affair. Ironically, this prevented his moving onward from the love of Socrates to the love of wisdom, up Diotima's ladder of erotic refinement. But what does the failed seduction say about Socrates? Hasn't he claimed (177d) to be an expert on Eros, and to have "fallen in love" with Alcibiades (213d)? Why would he then refuse to yield to the advances of this younger and more beautiful partner? Alcibiades gives a very striking answer to this question, claiming that our usual picture of Socrates, what we infer from his behavior, is all wrong and that in fact there is a continual deception endemic to Socrates' nature: "For you must understand that none of you knows the man." Both of Socrates' usual claims, to know nothing (see *Apology*) and to be erotically disposed toward handsome youths (see *Charmides*) are deceptive, Alcibiades explains. He *seems* to be ignorant, and *seems* to be erotically moved by physical beauty, "and this is how he goes around on the outside, just like that carved Silenus; but on the inside, once opened up, how full do you think he is, O my drinking companions, of self-restraint?" (216d). And more pointedly: "Beauty.... wealth ... he believes that all these attainments are worth nothing, and that we—you all, I tell you—amount to nothing; but throughout his life he is ironical, and he toys with people to the end" (216d). If this is so, Alcibiades can thrill the symposium with his racy story and yet save himself from the dishonor of having failed to seduce Socrates. We learned from Pausanias that seducing another man is honorable only if it works; to risk it and then flop is a matter for shame. As Alcibiades reminded us, he usually is not vulnerable to that emotion, and as he explains here, nobody need feel ashamed for failing to do the impossible.

Alcibiades reveals his special insight about Socrates with some hesitation, comparing the experience of Socratic irony to the agony of snakebite (217e). Both make us reluctant to discuss our experience with those who have not endured the same thing, he explains. This will readily remind us of the ceremonial religious mysteries that Alcibiades was accused of revealing to the uninitiated, especially when he urges "the slaves and whoever else of base and uncivilized character to pull closed the great doors of their ears" (218b) lest they hear what they should not.

SHAME BEFORE THE WISE

Earlier in the symposium, at 194b, we heard Agathon declare the importance of distinguishing between the judgment of the ignorant masses and the judgment of the wise few. Among Plato's motives for introducing this distinction was the desire to frustrate conventional justifications of paiderasty that Plato apparently found Sophistical and misleading. "If you thought yourself to be doing something shameful before the many," Socrates asks Agathon at 194c10, "wouldn't you be ashamed before them?" The context here is theater and the relevant questions about art and taste, but the rhetoric reminds us of Pausanias's speech on the limitations of popular mores. There, we learned the central tenet of paiderastic ideology: that the many are not fit to judge the actions of the right-thinking elite. Socrates seems to demolish that position in his exchange with Agathon.

As Alcibiades' story continues, we learn that he tried just such an argument on the philosopher at the crucial moment of his attempt at seduction: "I indeed would be much more ashamed before the wise for failing to [sexually] indulge such a man [as you, Socrates], than I would be ashamed before the many and the foolish for indulging him" (218d4). Given Socrates' freedom from the claims of popular praise and dispraise, it is no wonder that he was unmoved by such a suggestion. The speeches of Phaedrus and Pausanias constitute a sort of basic course in paiderastic ideology, a course that some of Plato's readers (say, remote foreigners or remote posterity) may need if they are to recognize Alcibiades' seduction story as laced with ironic plays upon the conventions of that subculture. "So I was with him, we two alone together, and I expected him immediately to begin conversing with me the way a lover [*erastês*] does with a youth [*paidikois*] when they're alone; and I was rejoicing. But no such thing happened ..." (217b5). A moment later, once these expectations have failed him, Alcibiades tries reversing the roles: "I invited him to dinner, just like a lover attempting a youth" (217d). Eventually it becomes clear to Alcibiades that nothing will work, and Socrates' refusal is the famous passage we discussed earlier: "look closer, lest it escape your notice that I am nothing" (219a2).

ANECDOTES OF SOCRATES' PRODIGIOUS POWERS OF ENDURANCE AT POTIDAEA AND DELIUM

In our discussion of Diotima's speech, we looked ahead to the speech of Alcibiades and considered his stories about Socrates' strange habits and abilities. These stories follow immediately upon the story of the failed seduction, and I have suggested that part of Alcibiades' point is to explain one piece of strange behavior (the refusal to gratify Alcibiades, who was regarded as the most handsome man of his generation) by pointing to others. Plato's point in telling these stories is of course more elaborate, and it leaves his readers with considerable interpretive work. At Potidaea, Socrates endured hunger better than any other person could; he was not eager to drink, but when compelled, he out drank everyone without ever appearing drunk; then he slighted the bitter cold weather by going about barefoot; later on the same campaign, during the summer, he sank deep into thought and remained motionless on the spot from one morning till the next, while the army, though intrigued, left him undisturbed. As for the fighting, at Potidaea Socrates saved the life of the wounded Alcibiades and then refused to be decorated for his feat. At Delium, his calmness and courage in retreat surpassed even that of the general, Laches (who figures in Plato's dialogue on courage, which bears his name).

SOCRATES AS AN ODYSSEUS FIGURE

Much has been made of these anecdotes, and the least of the observations we can make seems to be that Socrates is, as Alcibiades said at 216d, "full of *sophrosunê*," an important word usually translated as "self-control" or "temperance." This is the quality that Odysseus possessed and exercised with such striking consistency. The word is a compound of the verb root *so* (save), the noun *phren* (heart), and the abstract suffix *sune* (-ness). "Save-heart-ness" is the quality by which one preserves oneself intact: one emerges from any situation with one's physical and emotional integrity undiminished. It is natural to think of Odysseus when this characteristic of Socrates is being praised, especially since Odysseus has been invoked several times in *Symposium* thus far—and quite recently, at 220c, when Alcibiades introduced a story about Socrates with *Odyssey* 4.242, "here's another exploit the unconquerable man performed," which refers to Odysseus. Curiously, Alcibiades finishes his speech with a tribute to Socrates' uniqueness, explicitly rejecting the idea of an Homeric parallel:

> [T]here is no one like him at all, neither among those of the past nor among those now living; this is what merits the utmost amazement. For, to the sort of man that Achilles was, one might compare Brasidas and others, and to Pericles' kind, both Nestor and Antenor; and there are others besides, and one might make more such comparisons to other men: but this person, and his uncanniness [*atopia*], both himself and his arguments—one could search and find nobody even close, neither among those now living nor among the people of the past—unless one were to do as I have done, and compare him not to a human but to the Silenoi and the Satyrs, both him and his arguments. (221c4–d6)

That is what Alcibiades says (Nussbaum's rendering is particularly good here: "you could look and look and find no one even near him"

[167]), though as I have suggested, there is one Homeric hero who seems at least partly apt for the comparison, and readers may wonder why this comparison is not developed more explicitly. The answer seems to be in the special generic nature of the dialogue form. Plato wrote dialogues instead of treatises because he wanted his readers to come to their own conclusions, and the passages that seem like advocacy of one or another point of view almost invariably turn out to be caught in a productive tension with other passages. Plato may have chosen this genre solely for its pedagogical effectiveness, but the dialogues themselves are so rich in compelling yet competing arguments as to make us regard Plato himself as a fundamentally dialogic thinker, undecided about many of the great issues he articulated. Plato's project is generally understood as a revision of the Athenian culture he inherited, a culture dominated by Homer's epic poems and the emulation of the heroic models found therein. Part of the intelligibility of that project is Plato's revisionary borrowing from the same epic tradition with which he continually struggles. Socrates is like Odysseus, because both men emerge intact from situations that seduce and destroy those who lack *sophrosunê*; because both *Odyssey* and *Symposium* end with the *nostos* or homecoming of the hero; because each of these two heroes is awed by the beauty of a younger, potential sexual partner who makes erotic claims upon him (Alcibiades is to Socrates as Nausicaa is to Odysseus, in this limited respect) that he ironically refuses to gratify. But Socrates is also unlike Odysseus, because he prefers to ascend into the divine heights urged by Diotima's instruction, whereas Odysseus preferred the immanent, natural human charms of his mortal wife and refused the immortality offered by Calypso.[5]

ALCIBIADES' WARNING TO SOCRATES' ADMIRERS

Alcibiades finishes by talking about Socrates' characteristic arguments concerning the crafts (metallurgy, shoemaking, etc.—the kind of practical arts to which we find Socrates referring, for illustration, throughout the Platonic corpus). These arguments seem laughable at first, but they turn out to share Socrates' own resemblance to the hollow statues that Alcibiades explained earlier. Open up these arguments, and you find "many and divine effigies of virtue ... and everything one needs to contemplate if one is to become noble and good." So Alcibiades apparently still believes that Socrates has the power to improve people—but then the real ending of his speech occurs:

> Those are, men, the things I say in praise of Socrates—although, mixing it in, I also told you how I blame him for the way he abused [*hubrisen*] me. And furthermore, it isn't to me alone that he's done these things, but also to Charmides the son of Glaucon, and Euthydemus the son of Diocles, and many others, whom this man has deceived [by behaving] as an *erastês*—[but then] becoming rather the *paidika* instead of the *erastês*.[6] And indeed I'm telling you, Agathon, don't be deceived by him; take careful thought from our sufferings, and do not, as the proverb says, learn only after having suffered yourself, like a child. (222a7–b7)

Alcibiades said earlier (216d) that Socrates is continually deceiving everyone, on two counts: (a) he professes ignorance, though in fact he is full of everything necessary to the person who wants to become noble and good (a viable definition of wisdom), and (b) he behaves as though he is erotically moved by young men, though in fact he spurns them.[7] If this is Socrates' ongoing deception, what must these unfortunate young men have thought of it in order to have become its victims? Such persons would have to (a) *disbelieve* Socrates' claim to ignorance, since as we have seen in the cases of both Agathon and Alcibiades, their interest in Socrates was partly based on the hope of being made wise by him, and (b) at the same time they would have to *believe* Socrates' verbal and nonverbal claims to being infatuated with their own youthful beauty. In other words, becoming the dupe of Socratic "hubris" requires that one is by turns skeptical and credulous, and always in accord with one's own (apparent) self-interest. Since this kind of self-interest (the kind that prevents one from seeing the truth) is one of the things Socrates is out to critique, it makes sense that he should conduct himself in a way that frustrates this trait in his friends.

Return to the scene of Alcibiades' attempt. Here is Socrates' complete response:

> O my dear Alcibiades, you may prove formidable yet [or more literally, "you run the risk/ have a chance, of not being insignificant"], if what you say concerning me happens to be true indeed, and there is some power in me through which you might be improved. You must see in me a beauty entirely surpassing [or, entirely different from] your own. If indeed you're looking to strike a bargain between yourself and me, and you try to make an exchange of beauty for beauty, you intend to cheat me by no small amount: you're trying to acquire the truth [*aletheia*] of what's beautiful in exchange for opinion [*doxês*] about what's beautiful [that is, you're trying to acquire the reality of beauty (Socrates' wisdom) in exchange for the mere appearance of beauty (Alcibiades' good looks)]; you really intend "to exchange gold for bronze."[8] But, O blessed one, examine better, lest it escape your notice that I am nothing [that is, I count for little, have nothing to offer]. For the sight of the mind begins to see sharply, when the sight of the eyes has begun to decline from its peak [that is, its peak of youth and health]; and you're still far from that point. (218d7–219a4)

The phrase "O blessed one" is not especially religious language in the original; it is Socrates' ironic praise of Alcibiades' prodigious natural endowments, of which the most relevant is his handsomeness—that ephemeral "bronze" that Socrates will not accept in exchange for his own intellectual "gold." The verb in this injunction, "examine [*skopei*] better, O blessed one," generally meant "look," and Plato was largely responsible for extending the range of this and many other words to include a more or less new, intellectual sense; here "look" means "consider, examine, contemplate."[9] The rhetoric of vision pervades the whole passage, as it pervaded Diotima's discourse, because it was already prominent in the esoteric Mysteries of Eleusis—Plato's model for both Diotima's esoteric Beauty and Alcibiades' esoteric Socrates. Here at 219a, we have a further link between those two esoteric visions: the old man's gently chiding remark mentions "the sight of the mind," and how our mental vision becomes sharp only when youthful beauty is gone and the "sight of the eyes" has begun to fail. This mental sight is just the faculty Diotima has in mind at 212a; it is "that by which it is necessary to gaze upon" the Beautiful itself.

11

The Epilogue

THE TRAGIC AND COMIC POET

Aristophanes and Agathon were next to one another in the sequence of speakers only because of the former's bout of hiccups. The expected order, *Aristophanes—Eryximachus—Agathon,* was changed when the first two men had to trade turns and let the comic poet's hiccups run their course. The resulting order, *Eryximachus—Aristophanes—Agathon,* puts the comic poet next to the recently victorious tragic one. It is Plato's quite deliberate artifice in this matter that calls our attention to it, and we wonder what it may mean, until we reach the end of *Symposium,* where we find the following issue singled out for scrutiny:

> Aristodemus said ... that waking up towards dawn, the cocks already crowing, he saw that the others were asleep, or had gone, but only Agathon, Aristophanes, and Socrates were still awake, drinking from a big vessel and passing it around from the right. And so Socrates was conversing with them. Aristodemus said he didn't remember the rest of their conversation, having been asleep, and therefore not present from the beginning; but the

general heading of it was, he said, that Socrates compelled them
to agree that the same man who knows how to make comedy also
knows how to make tragedy, and he who is a tragic poet by means
of his art, is also a comic poet. And they were indeed compelled
by these things—not following very zealously, being sleepy; and
Aristophanes went to sleep first, and then, when dawn came,
Agathon. (223c2–d8)

In his speech in praise of Eros, Socrates often assimilated apparently
diverse things into an underlying unity: what look like different kinds
of affinities are really just the same eros but attached to diverse pur-
suits and objects (205d); or again, there are diverse beauties to be
found here in the world of daily life, but they all turn out to derive
their beauty from a single ultimate source, the Beautiful itself (211).
Here at the dialogue's end, Socrates is making a similar move: tragedy
and comedy may seem to be utterly distinct, but the selfsame faculty is
responsible for their making. Therefore, whoever possesses this faculty must be capable (at least in principle) of making both kinds of
poetry, even if he can only be found making one kind. Aristophanes
the comedian and Agathon the tragedian are "compelled to agree"
with this, as Alcibiades was compelled to agree that he was not yet
ready for public life. It is not what they want to hear, and they give
their assent while "not following very zealously." The fall into sleep
comes just at the limits of the artistic repertoire each writer has
already mastered; but Socrates, as a nonlover and nonwriter, committed to no artistic genre and no erotic partner, outlasts everyone and
goes soberly home to bathe:

And so Socrates, having brought them down to sleep, stood up to
go; and just as was usual, Aristodemus followed; and he went into
the Lyceum [a sanctuary of Apollo, with a garden and a gymna-
sium], bathed, and just as on any other day, he held conversation,
and so conversing until evening, he got up and went home.
(223d8–d12)

Plato, on the contrary, was indeed a writer, and he wrote this strangely
versatile kind of drama called Socratic dialogue. The philosophy
exemplified and celebrated in the Platonic corpus labors toward a

happy outcome for humanity, rescuing us from the darkness of ignorance and holding out hope that we may someday become wise, and
even immortal. Yet this same body of work makes us mourn for a
world that we, like Plato himself, have lost: a world of earliness and
innovation and youthful promise, torn by war and faction, but (until
399 B.C.E.) still strong enough to tolerate the friend whom Plato
loved.

Notes and References

Chronology

1. Charles Rowan Beye. *Greek Literature and Society*. Ithaca, N.Y.: Cornell University Press, 1987.

2. This is the date suggested by Martha C. Nussbaum in *The Fragility of Goodness: Luck and Ethics in Greek Tragedy and Philosophy* (Cambridge: Cambridge University Press, 1986; hereafter cited in text) as part of an account that I find generally persuasive. Although I favor it on balance, one disadvantage of the Nussbaum date is that it does not agree with Apollodorus's casual remark at 173b7, "The road into town is utterly serviceable for those walking, to talk and to listen," since in 404 B.C.E. the Spartan occupation should have made that road less than serviceable. But the choice between this date and the more usually accepted 401/400 B.C.E. does not much affect my argument, and the most important date for *Symposium* is not this disputed date of the frame story (in which Apollodorus converses with the stranger) but the date of the drinking party, 416 B.C.E., upon which all readers agree.

1. Historical Context

1. H. D. F. Kitto, *The Greeks* (Baltimore, Md.: Penguin, 1951), 107; hereafter cited in text.

2. Victor Ehrenberg, *From Solon to Socrates* (London: Methuen, 1967), 134; hereafter cited in text.

3. In this connection, it is worth remembering that Athenian military ambition was part of what the tragedian Sophocles had in mind when he warned, in *Oedipus Tyrannus*, "Hubris, if it gorges on abundance, in vain, against the moment and the circumstance...it mounts up to the highest, stepping from the precipice to ruin, where the footsteps cannot help" (lines 873-79). Pericles was not against Athenian expansionism per se, but he warned

that the Empire should minimize the risks of new conquest by waiting for a propitious shift in the regional balance of power.

4. Thucydides, 3.87; Ehrenberg, 264.

5. Plutarch, *The Rise and Fall of Athens: Nine Greek Lives*, trans. Ian Scott-Kilvert (London: Penguin, 1960), 284.

6. This commonplace can be found in, for example, Eric Havelock, *Preface to Plato*, 2d ed. (New York: Grosset and Dunlap, 1967), hereafter cited in text; and Moses Hadas, *The Greek Ideal and Its Survival* (New York: Harper and Row, 1960), hereafter cited in text as Hadas 1960.

7. "Hellenistic" refers to the Greek culture of the era that began with the death of Alexander in 323 B.C.E.

8. See, for example, Kitto, 218–19.

9. One of the high points of this controversial enthusiasm for rhetoric was the arrival in Athens, in 427 B.C.E., of the famous Sophist Gorgias of Leontini. His influence can be heard in the speech of Agathon.

10. For more on this issue and on Sophism in general, see George Kerferd, *The Sophistic Movement* (Cambridge: Cambridge University Press, 1981), hereafter cited in text.

11. Note that in *Republic, dialectic* comes to refer to the whole process by which knowledge accrues to the learner, a process that, even in *Republic,* still *begins with* question and answer (since that kind of discourse is best for negating and removing the false wisdom that would otherwise crowd out real wisdom). After the *elenchos*—cross-examination by negative question and answer—Plato constructs various ladders to positive knowledge, mainly in middle-period dialogues like *Phaedrus* and *Symposium.*

12. Moses Hadas, *Ancilla to Classical Reading* (New York: Columbia University Press, 1954), 129.

13. There is one traditional exception to the statement that Socrates did not write: at *Phaedo* 60c–61b Plato tells us that, near the time of his execution, Socrates wrote a hymn to Apollo and a poetic version of some of Aesop's fables. We need not doubt this, although no such writings have survived.

14. The word *metaphysics* is not as old as the pre-Socratic writers I am now discussing, but it was they who framed many of the issues that came to comprise the conceptual purview of metaphysics.

15. *Ion,* 536a.

16. This is the theme of Nussbaum's important study of Greek ethics, *The Fragility of Goodness.* That book's chapter on *Symposium* has influenced the present study, not least by the insight it affords into the relationship between the issues of this section, "Historical Context" and those of the later section, "A Reading."

2. Critical Reception

1. Stanley Rosen seems to have been the first person to make this emphatically clear, in the 1968 edition of his monograph, *Plato's Symposium* (2d ed. [New Haven, Conn.: Yale University Press, 1987], 337; hereafter cited in text).

2. Ian Mueller, "Mathematical Method and Philosophical Truth," in *The Cambridge Companion to Plato,* ed. Richard Kraut (Cambridge: Cambridge University Press, 1992), 170.

3. Gordon Leff, *Medieval Thought: Augustine to Ockham* (Baltimore, Md.: Penguin, 1958), 174.

4. For the Platonism of Percy Bysshe Shelley, see James Notopoulos, *The Platonism of Shelley: A Study of Platonism and the Poetic Mind* (Durham, N. C.: Duke University Press, 1949). For the Cambridge Platonists, see Gerald R. Cragg, ed., *The Cambridge Platonists* (Oxford: Oxford University Press, 1968).

5. For a stunningly succinct statement of Nietzsche's (1889) views on this issue, see "How the 'Real World' at last Became a Myth," in *Twilight of the Idols,* trans. R. J. Hollingdale (New York: Penguin, 1968), 40–41.

6. I use this spelling of the term *paiderasty* because it is closer to the Greek form and may help the reader to distinguish between the social phenomenon found in ancient Athens and any modern phenomena named in the standard English *pederasty.*

3. The Prologue (172a–174a)

1. See note 1 in the chronology. The alternative date, 401/400 B.C.E. comes from K. J. Dover, ed. *Plato: Symposium* (Cambridge: Cambridge University Press, 1980), hereafter cited in text as Dover 1980.

2. For more on the date, see K. J. Dover, "The Date of Plato's Symposium," *Phronesis* 10 (1965), and the introduction to Dover's Cambridge edition of the text; also, the first few pages of Nussbaum's *Symposium* chapter. For more on the dating of Plato's works in general, see Leonard Branwood, "Stylometry and Chronology" in *The Cambridge Companion to Plato,* ed. Richard Kraut (Cambridge: Cambridge University Press, 1992).

3. Gilbert Rose, *Plato's* Symposium, 2d ed. (Bryn Mawr, Pa.: Bryn Mawr Commentaries, 1985), 1; hereafter cited in text.

4. R. E. Allen gives the former reading ("first tragedy") in his translation, *The Dialogues of Plato,* vol. 2, *The Symposium* (New Haven, Conn.: Yale University Press, 1991), 112. The latter ("first victory") seems to be a minority reading, but it is quite clearly supported by Nussbaum's paraphrase of the passage (168) and by Rose in his commentary's preface (v).

5. Pickard-Cambridge, *Dramatic Festivals of Athens,* 2d ed. (Oxford: Oxford University Press, 1968), 41.

6. Odysseus is a good man coming uninvited to the feast of the bad Suitors, while their feast is rightfully his (the good man's) and they have come to it uninvited.

7. Ennis Rees, trans., *The Iliad of Homer* (London: Oxford University Press, 1963), 195–96.

8. This word *atopon* is formed from *topos* (place) and *a-*, the negation (called alpha privative in Greek grammar); whatever is *atopos* is "placeless, out of place" and so "strange" because unplaceable in any category. The word occurs three times in *Symposium*: the first time, it describes Socrates' session of intense concentration in the doorway of Agathon's neighbor (175a10); the second, the way all human knowledge constantly flows away and is replaced (207e5); the last, the figure of Socrates in general (215a2).

9. Further information and discussion of these issues can be found in K. J. Dover, *Greek Homosexuality,* 2d ed. (Cambridge, Mass.: Harvard University Press, 1989); David Halperin, John J. Winkler, and Froma Zeitlin, eds., *Before Sexuality: The Construction of Erotic Experience in the Ancient Greek World* (Princeton, N.J.: Princeton University Press, 1990), hereafter cited in text as Halperin; and David Cohen, *Law, Sexuality, and Society: The Enforcement of Morals in Classical Athens* (Cambridge: Cambridge University Press, 1991), hereafter cited in text.

4. The Speech of Phaedrus: Praise and Blame

1. See Cohen, 186: "In Athens, agonistic sexuality could scarcely manifest itself in the competition for women for a variety of reasons. First, institutionalized courtship of unmarried women was non-existent, and clandestine courtship was difficult and somewhat impractical, since girls were married very young to prevent just such 'accidents' and were zealously guarded during the brief period between adolescence and marriage ... Adulterous unions were an attractive option to some men, but fraught with danger."

2. See John J. Winkler, "Laying Down The Law: The Oversight of Men's Sexual Behavior in Classical Athens," in Halperin, 178, 186.

3. Dover's explanation for this makes sense: the lover is, says Phaedrus, full of the god [Eros], so the gods "naturally react favorably" to the beloved's reverence of what is, after all, divine (Dover 1980, 95). But part of Phaedrus's meaning must also be that it is simply more amazing, whether to the gods or anyone else, when the younger and more beautiful party loves the older and less beautiful.

4. At least, Phaedrus is seated next to him at *Protagoras* 315c, and is "used to being persuaded by you [Eryximachus], especially when you talk of

medical matters," at *Symposium* 176d; also, they appear to leave together at the end of the symposium, 223b7. Finally, Phaedrus and Eryximachus were both named as participants in the religious crimes of 416 B.C.E. (see the section in chapter 1 on Alcibiades' career). Whether his *erastês* is indeed Eryximachus, Phaedrus certainly regards himself as an *eromenos*.

5. The Speech of Pausanias: A Sophisticated Relativism

1. Two important books on the cultural entailments of the orality/literacy issue are Walter Ong, *Orality and Literacy* (London: Methuen, 1982) and Havelock

2. Prodicus B7, quoted in Dover 1980, 2.

3. That is, sexual conquest and eventual orgasm.

4. Martin Luther, "The Freedom of A Christian," in John Dillenberger, ed., *Martin Luther: Selections from His Writings* (New York: Anchor Books, 1958).

6. The Speech of Eryximachus: Medicine and Love

1. I have modified Robin Waterfield's translation here.

2. Charles H. Kahn, *The Art and Thought of Heraclitus* (Cambridge: Cambridge University Press, 1979), 64–65, 195–200.

7. The Speech of Aristophanes: The Yearning for Wholeness

1. Harold Bloom, *The Anxiety of Influence* (New York: Oxford University Press, 1973*)*.

8. The Speech of Agathon: Eros as a Young, Beautiful Poet

1. A notable exception to this, and to the general contempt in which the Sophists have been held since antiquity, is Kerferd.

2. This quotation, "the Nomoi are the city's king," is said by Aristotle to have come from a rhetorician named Alcidamas.

3. In the fragment of Sophocles from which this quotation comes, it is Necessity (rather than Eros) who is too powerful for Ares.

4. Jesus, for instance, uses a fortiori arguments quite often; for example, Matt. 6:26.

5. This is echoed in Saint Augustine, *On The Teacher*: "Who is so foolishly curious as to send his child to school in order to learn what the teacher thinks?" (J. H. S. Burleigh, ed., *Augustine: Earlier Writings* [Philadelphia: Westminster, 1953], 100).

9. The Speech of Socrates: Diotima, the Itinerant Priestess, Explains Eros

1.   This is part of the warrant for the very reasonable view, held by a variety of critics (e.g., F. M. Cornford, "The Doctrine of Eros in Plato's *Symposium*," in *Plato II: A Collection of Critical Essays,* ed. Gregory Vlastos [Notre Dame, Ind.: Notre Dame University Press, 1971]), which holds that there was no historical "Diotima of Mantinea," but that Socrates (either at a real, historical moment or only here in Plato's *Symposium*) invented her as a mouthpiece for his own views in order to avoid the claim that he knew more about Eros than did his host. That claim would have been impolite and, given Socrates' usual claim to ignorance (mentioned by Alcibiades at 216d), inconsistent.

2.   The Greek idiom here is *genesthai autô,* an infinitive of *gignomai* (become), with the personal pronoun *autô* in the dative of possession: the lover of beautiful things desires that those things "should come to be *to him*"; that is, be his. It may be that Plato used this idiom here, rather than a simple verb of possession like *echein,* in order to suggest that there is a generativity already operative in this simple desire for beautiful things. "Procreation in the beautiful" is the theme toward which we are headed, a theme Plato often expresses with forms of this same verb *gignomai*; see, for instance, 209a–210.

3.   The Greek here is difficult, and of the translations I have consulted, that of R. E. Allen seems to me to be the most correct. My own rendering of this passage is indebted to Allen's.

4.   Again, as Dover (1980) points out in his note on this passage, the poetry of Plato's word choice suggests the erotic nature of philosophy: the verb for Socrates' coming to Diotima, *phoitân,* means "to go regularly," used of children going to school but also of persons in an episodic but continuous sexual relationship.

5.   This word, *skuthrôpon,* means "frown, look angry or sullen." A translator could emphasize the *difficulty* of birth-amid-the-ugly by saying that in it the pregnant one "grimaces," or, instead, one could emphasize the way this very difficulty *delays* the birth, by saying that he or she "broods."

6.   "The pregnancy is very difficult to bear." The sense is that the pregnancy is difficult to *deliver,* and so much so that there is no delivery yet, which makes the protracted pregnancy difficult to *endure.* Incidentally, this is part of the problem among the Theban population before Oedipus comes out to fix things; see Sophocles, *Oedipus Tyrannus,* lines 171–74.

7.   Ending the pains by mitigating them, but also by ending the labor, at last, in delivery.

8.   Michael Morgan, *Platonic Piety: Philosophy and Ritual in Fourth Century Athens* (New Haven, Conn.: Yale University Press, 1987).

9. The verb of looking, which occurs here and elsewhere in Diotima's discourse, is *theorein,* from which we get the word *theory.* In Plato's usage, it is an intellectual gazing, with what *Republic* 533d calls "the eye of the soul." This is why "contemplation" is an adequate rendering of it.

10. A more literal rendering would be "for the acquiring of this possession," but the Greek word *ktesis* can also mean "success" in an endeavor, and the English *achieve* can also mean "acquire" (e.g., "Bid them achieve me and then sell my bones," Shakespeare, *Henry V,* 4.3.127). I think the ambiguity is productive, since it shows Plato quite characteristically stretching the meanings of the available words.

11. 212b6, *ta erotika ... diapherontôs askô.* The adverb can mean "surpassingly, bearing through to the end," from *dia* (through) and *pherô* (to carry); but it can also mean "differently." So the phrase "I practice erotics *diapherontôs*" can either affirm Socrates' unswerving commitment to the practice of precisely Diotima's teaching, or it can indicate that he practices erotics *differently* from the way she instructed—which would help explain his refusal of Alcibiades' erotic advances in 219.

12. The ladder image occurs in the Torah at Genesis 28:12 and in the Koran at 17:1, but its considerable importance in the mystical traditions of Judaism, Christianity, and Islam seems to have come about via Plotinus and Neoplatonism. A brief and illuminating survey of the history of the ladder image after Plotinus is Alexander Altmann, "The Ladder of Ascension," in his *Studies in Religious Philosophy and Mysticism* (Ithaca, N.Y.: Cornell University Press, 1969). Irma Brandeis's 1960 study of this topos in Dante, *The Ladder of Vision* (New York: Doubleday), remains important.

13. This observation has been enabled by a similar argument about the Persian *Thousand and One Nights,* in Fedwa Malti-Douglas, *Woman's Body, Woman's Word: Gender and Discourse in Arabo-Islamic Writing* (Princeton, N.J.: Princeton University Press, 1991).

10. The Speech of Alcibiades: Socrates the Inscrutable

1. At this point one might hear echoes of the Cyclops episode in Homer's *Odyssey,* in which the monster who has no respect for the gods, or for proper guest-host relationships, drinks enormous amounts of unmixed wine, only to be requited for all that hubristic behavior by the cruel cleverness of Odysseus. The point is that excessive drinking, particularly of *unmixed* wine, is hubristic; like the Cyclops, Alcibiades drinks this way *and* disrespects the gods (or was accused of so doing; see chapter 1). As Odysseus triumphed over the Cyclops by calling himself *outis* (nobody), Socrates will elude Alcibiades with the remark, "look well, lest it elude you that I am nothing [*ouden ôn*]."

2. Marsyas was a flute-playing satyr who challenged Apollo to a competition, lost, and was flayed alive as punishment for this hubris.

3. Such an idea is developed in Havelock (especially chapter 11). Søren Kierkegaard's doctoral thesis, *The Concept of Irony: With Continual Reference to Socrates* suggests something similar, on rather different grounds; see the translation by Howard Hong and Edna Hong in the 1989 Princeton University Press edition of *Kierkegaard's Writings*, vol. 2.

4. Late in his life Plato wrote an essay, "To the Friends and Associates of Dion," describing the early part of his development. "When I was young my experience was the same as that of many others. I thought as soon as I became my own master I would immediately enter into public life. But it so happened, that...." The essay goes on to explain how political events brought Plato to withdraw from public affairs and to turn to philosophy for the wisdom that political activity demanded but could not supply. (Translation in Paul Friedländer, *Plato: An Introduction,* trans. Hans Meyerhoff [New York: Harper, 1958], 3–5).

5. For a survey of the Platonic linkage between Socrates and Odysseus in *Republic,* see Jacob Howland's volume on that dialogue in the present series: *The Republic: The Odyssey of Philosophy* (New York: Twayne, 1993), chapter 5.

6. A possible secondary sense of this line is "whom this man has deceived as an erastês, [but then] being the paidika himself, resisting against an erastês."

7. Diotima (at 211d) lends support to the claim that Socrates is often overwhelmed by the beauty of young men. See also *Charmides* and *Protagoras.*

8. This is a quotation of Homer, *Iliad* 4.236, in which Glaucus trades his golden armor for the bronze armor of Diomedes. That exchange became, as it is here, proverbial for a one-sided bargain. In the present case, Socrates says that Alcibiades is planning to exchange Socrates' gold (wisdom) for Alcibiades' own bronze (bodily loveliness and sexual favors).

9. It is often pointed out that the word *theory* comes from another Greek verb of seeing, *theorein*; this development, like so much of the Western philosophical lexicon, is largely due to Plato.

Selected Bibliography

Primary Texts

Dover, K. J., ed. *Plato: Symposium.* Cambridge: Cambridge University Press, 1980.

Kahn, Charles, ed. *The Art and Thought of Heraclitus.* Cambridge: Cambridge University Press, 1979.

MacDowell, Douglas M., ed. *Andokides: On the Mysteries.* New York: Oxford University Press, 1962.

Rees, Ennis, trans. *The Iliad of Homer.* London: Oxford University Press, 1963.

Translations

Allen, R. E. *The Dialogues of Plato.* Vol. 2, *Symposium.* New Haven, Conn.: Yale University Press, 1991. Contains a fine translation, less literary than Waterfield but closer to the Greek in its expression. Also contains a commentary.

Hamilton, Walter, trans. *Plato: The Symposium.* London: Penguin, 1951. A readable rendering with a helpful introduction.

Waterfield, Robin, trans. *Plato's Symposium.* New York: Oxford University Press, 1994. Mellifluous and generally accurate rendering into modern English idiom. Includes useful notes and a glossary. More informative than Hamilton.

Secondary Texts
Classical Greek History and Society

Beye, Charles Rowan. *Ancient Greek Literature and Society.* Ithaca, N.Y.: Cornell University Press, 1987. An illuminating survey of important developments.

Burkert, Walter. *Greek Religion.* Trans. John Raffan. Cambridge, Mass.: Harvard University Press, 1985. An important account of the evolving consensus on Greek religion, to which Burkert himself has been a major contributor.

Cohen, David. *Law, Sexuality, and Society: The Enforcement of Morals in Classical Athens.* Cambridge: Cambridge University Press, 1991. This book builds on the work of Dover and Michel Foucault to make a sophisticated and insightful review of the evidence.

Dover, K. J. *Greek Homosexuality,* 2d ed. Cambridge, Mass.: Harvard University Press, 1989. The definitive work on the complex issues of homosexuality in Classical Greece.

Ehrenberg, Victor. *From Solon to Socrates.* London: Methuen, 1967. The special merit of this history is its readability.

Hadas, Moses. *The Greek Ideal and Its Survival.* New York: Harper and Row, 1960. Moses Hadas was a master teacher and translator. This brief work provides an overview of the legacy of Hellenism.

Halperin, David, John J. Winkler, and Froma Zeitlin, eds. *Before Sexuality: The Construction of Erotic Experience in the Ancient Greek World.* Princeton, N.J.: Princeton University Press, 1990. A collection of essays with adept treatments of difficult issues including the ancient gynecology and reproductive physiology.

Kerferd, George. *The Sophistic Movement.* Cambridge: Cambridge University Press, 1981. Argues that the Sophists were serious and profound thinkers and explores the way Platonic ideology has obscured the scholarly perception of the Sophists since antiquity.

Kitto, H. D. F. *The Greeks.* Baltimore, Md.: Penguin, 1951. Still a fine introduction to the classical period.

Pomeroy, Sarah. *Goddesses, Whores, Wives, and Slaves: Women in Classical Antiquity.* New York: Schocken, 1975. The first full-length treatment of the status of women in the classical world. Remains illuminating and important.

Stockton, David. *The Classical Athenian Democracy.* Oxford: Oxford University Press, 1990. A readable survey of the development of Greek political institutions.

Vernant, Jean-Pierre, and Vidal Naquet. *Myth and Tragedy in Ancient Greece.* New York: Zone Books, 1990. A compelling investigation of Greek tragedy, especially Sophocles, with attention to historical and sociological aspects.

Socrates and Plato

Ficino, Marsilio. *Commentary on Plato's Symposium.* Ed. and trans. Jayne Sears. Bears a sometimes tenuous relationship to Plato's dialogue, but exemplifies an important historical moment in Renaissance Platonism.

Friedländer, Paul. *Plato: An Introduction.* Trans. Hans Meyerhoff. New York: Harper, 1958. A classic continental account of the major issues in Plato.

Havelock, Eric. *Preface to Plato,* 2d ed. New York: Grosset and Dunlap, 1967. Despite the salient and incisive criticism of Leo Strauss, this book remains a useful introduction to the intellectual change brought about by the gradual dominance of the written word, exemplified by Plato, over the oral tradition of Homeric poetry.

Howland, Jacob. *The Republic: The Odyssey of Philosophy.* New York: Twayne, 1993. A fine introductory treatment to Plato's *Republic,* with attention to Homeric influence.

Kierkegaard, Søren. *The Concept of Irony: With Continual Reference to Socrates.* 1841. Trans. Howard Hong and Edna Hong. Princeton, N.J.: Princeton University Press, 1989. The philosopher's doctoral thesis. Contains passages of striking insight into Socratic thought.

Kraut, Richard, ed. *The Cambridge Companion to Plato.* Cambridge: Cambridge University Press, 1992. Contains highly useful introductory essays on important aspects of Plato's corpus, including stylometry, the historical milieu, the dialogue form, and Platonic love.

Morgan, Michael. *Platonic Piety: Philosophy and Ritual in Fourth Century Athens.* New Haven, Conn.: Yale University Press, 1987. Explicates the role of Athenian religion and ritual in Plato's argumentation.

Nietzsche, Friedrich. *Twilight of the Idols.* 1889. Trans. R. J. Hollingdale. New York: Penguin, 1968. Strident but illuminating critique of Western thought, especially the legacy of Platonism.

Novotný, František. *The Posthumous Life of Plato.* Trans. Jana Fábryová. Prague: Publishing House of the Czech Academy of Sciences, 1977. A superb investigation of the history of Platonism and the myriad philosophical projects to which it has contributed. This book is hard to find, and an enterprising person might well get into heaven by bringing this book back into print.

Nussbaum, Martha C. *The Fragility of Goodness: Luck and Ethics in Greek Tragedy and Philosophy.* Cambridge: Cambridge University Press, 1986. Reads philosophical and literary texts together, drawing important conclusions about the human condition.

Rose, Gilbert. *Plato's Symposium.* 2d ed. Bryn Mawr, Pa.: Bryn Mawr Commentaries, 1985. A helpful guide to reading the Greek text of *Symposium.* Useful with Dover's edition.

Rosen, Stanley. *Plato's Symposium,* 2d ed. New Haven, Conn.: Yale University Press, 1987. An important, full-length monograph that draws out the political implications of the speeches while making a variety of original inferences.

Vlastos, Gregory. *Plato II: A Collection of Critical Essays.* Notre Dame, Ind.: University of Notre Dame Press, 1971. Contains helpful and sometimes historically important arguments.

Vander Waerdt, Paul. *The Socratic Movement.* Ithaca, N.Y.: Cornell University Press, 1994. As though influenced by Kerferd, examines Socrates and his circle as a social-intellectual phenomenon in Athens. Attention is given to Aristophanes, Plato, Xenophon, and some less frequently discussed figures like Aeschines.

Index

The Author

Jamey Hecht is assistant professor of English at Castleton State College, Vermont. He received his Ph.D. from Brandeis University and studied Greek at the Latin-Greek Institute, City University of New York. He has published scholarly articles on diverse authors including Virgil, Thomas More, Keats, Whitman, and Melville, along with reviews of contemporary fiction, poetry, and theater. A verse translation of *Sophocles' Theban Plays* will appear from Wordsworth Editions, United Kingdom in 2002.

The Editor

Robert Lecker is professor of English at McGill University in Montreal. He received his Ph.D. from York University. Professor Lecker is the author of numerous critical studies, including *On the Line* (1982), *Robert Kroetch* (1986), *An Other I* (1988), and *Making It Real: The Canonization of English-Canadian Literature* (1995). He is the editor of the critical journal *Essays on Canadian Writing* and of many collections of critical essays, the most recent of which is *Canadian Canons: Essays in Literary Value* (1991). He is the founding and current general editor of Twayne's Masterwork Studies and the editor of the Twayne World Authors Series on Canadian writers. He is also the general editor of G. K. Hall's Critical Essays on World Literature series.